Cambridge Practice Tests for First Certificate 1 & 2

Paul Carne
Louise Hashemi and
Barbara Thomas

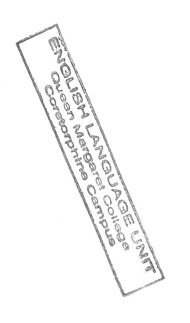

CAMBRIDGE
UNIVERSITY PRESS

PUBLISHED BY THE PRESS SYNDICATE OF THE UNIVERSITY OF CAMBRIDGE
The Pitt Building, Trumpington Street, Cambridge, United Kingdom

CAMBRIDGE UNIVERSITY PRESS
The Edinburgh Building, Cambridge CB2 2RU, UK   http://www.cup.cam.ac.uk
40 West 20th Street, New York, NY 10011–4211, USA   http://www.cup.org
10 Stamford Road, Oakleigh, Melbourne 3166, Australia
Ruiz de Alarcón 13, 28014 Madrid, Spain

First published 2000

Printed in the United Kingdom at the University Press, Cambridge

Typeface 10.5/12pt Sabon   *System* QuarkXPress® SE

ISBN 0 521 77422 5 Student's Book 1 & 2
ISBN 0 521 77423 3 Teacher's Book 1 & 2
ISBN 0 521 49898 8 Cassette Set (Book 1)
ISBN 0 521 49902 X Cassette Set (Book 2)

Overview of contents

To the student

The practice papers in this book are modelled on the papers of the University of Cambridge Local Examinations Syndicate (UCLES) **First Certificate in English** (FCE).

What is FCE?

The best-known group of Cambridge examinations for students of English as a foreign language are:

CPE – Certificate of Proficiency in English (very advanced)
CAE – Certificate in Advanced English
FCE – First Certificate in English
PET – Preliminary English Test
KET – Key English Test (elementary)

As you see, FCE is in the middle of the group. Passing FCE means that you are an 'independent user' of English. This means that you can use English with confidence in a variety of situations, even though you still have more to learn.

Using this book

You can use the practice tests in this book, with help from your English teacher, to:
● Judge the level of FCE to see whether it is the right examination for you.
● Get used to the kind of questions that you may meet in FCE, so that you can improve your accuracy and speed.
● Find out which papers you need most practice in.

These practice tests

This book contains eight complete practice tests. Each test has five papers, like this:

Paper 1   Reading (1 hour 15 minutes)

Each paper contains **four texts** taken from different newspapers, magazines, books and leaflets. There are **thirty-five questions** of different kinds, including multiple choice and multiple matching.
For examples, see Book 1 pp. 4–12.

Paper 2   Writing (1 hour 30 minutes)

Part 1: You **must answer** this section. You have to read some written material which gives information you need in your answer. You then write a **letter** of 120–180 words.
Part 2: You must **choose one** out of four writing tasks, and write 120–180 words. One of these tasks is about a book. The set books change every two

years but here are some examples of the kinds of books which might appear.
(Contact UCLES for the current list of set books – address on p.vi.)
The Go-Between by L. P. Hartley (simplified version)
Jamaica Inn by Daphne du Maurier (simplified version)
Brave New World by Aldous Huxley (Longman Bridge/Longman Fiction)
Crime Never Pays Oxford Bookworm Collections (OUP)
An Inspector Calls by J. B. Priestley
For examples of Paper 2 questions, see Book 1 pp. 13–16.

Paper 3 **Use of English** (1 hour 15 minutes)

You must answer all **five parts** of this paper. There are **sixty-five questions** and
all the answers are very short. This paper tests your knowledge of English
grammar, spelling and vocabulary, so accuracy is essential.
For examples, see Book 1 pp. 17–23.

Paper 4 **Listening** (about 40 minutes)

The listening test is recorded on tape and is divided into **four parts**. You have to
answer all **thirty questions**. Each text is heard **twice**. There are pauses on the
tape for you to read the questions and mark your answers. There are different
kinds of questions for each part.
For examples, see Book 1 pp. 24–28.

Paper 5 **Speaking** (14 minutes)

You take part in a conversation with another candidate and an examiner. There
is another examiner in the room who does not join in the conversation. During
the test the examiner will give you photographs and other pictures to look at
and talk about. Some of your conversation will be with the other candidate,
some with the examiner.

Beyond the classroom

Try to get as much practice as you can in English. Here are some suggestions to
help your studies in your own time.

Reading: Look out for English language magazines on subjects that interest you.
You may be surprised how much you understand!
Many English publishers produce simplified novels and short stories for
students of English as a foreign language. These are at different levels of
difficulty. Try reading some of these and perhaps other books in English
too. Modern thrillers are often good to start with. Above all, aim to
increase your reading speed and vocabulary.

Writing: If you have time, keep a daily diary in English; if not, what about once
a week? Get a penfriend somewhere in the English-speaking world, or
persuade a fellow student to exchange letters regularly. Whenever you
can, practise writing in English, so that you are used to it.

Listening: If you are not in an English-speaking country, find out about English-
language broadcasts in your area. Write to the BBC at Bush House, PO

Box 76, Strand, London WC2B 4PH, for details of their programmes in your part of the world. There may also be broadcasts from countries such as the USA or Australia which you can receive. If you enjoy music, look out for recordings of songs in English which have the words supplied with them. If you watch videos, try to get English-language versions of films.

Speaking: Try to practise speaking English as often as you can with your fellow students and with any English speakers you meet. You'll be surprised how much you can improve your spoken English through using it regularly.

Results

You will get a certificate when you pass the examination, showing your grade: A, B or C. A is the highest grade. You will also be informed if you do particularly well in any individual paper. D and E are failing grades. If you fail, you will be informed about which papers were your weakest.

Further information

For details about Cambridge examinations for students of English as a foreign language, write to:

EFL Division
UCLES
1 Hills Road
Cambridge
CB1 2EU
England.

Book 1 contents

Thanks

We are grateful to Jeanne McCarten, Elizabeth Sharman, Amanda Ogden and Peter Ducker of CUP for their hard work in helping us; to everyone at AVP Recording Studio and to all the people at UCLES who provided us with information.

The authors and publishers would also like to thank the teachers and students at the following institutions for piloting the material for us:

The Cheltenham School of English; The Bell Language School, Saffron Walden; The British Institute, Paris; Basil Paterson College, Edinburgh; Anglo Continental, Bournemouth; The British Institute, Florence; International House, Barcelona; Oxford House College, London.

Acknowledgements

The publishers are grateful to the following for permission to reproduce copyright material. It has not always been possible to identify sources of all the material used, and in such cases the publishers would welcome information from the copyright owners.

The Guardian/Observer for the articles on p.5 (*Life* magazine 3.4.94) and p.57 (*The Guardian* April 1986); New Crane Publishing Ltd for the article on p.6 (*Sainsbury's Magazine* March 1994); Lands' End Direct Merchants UK Ltd for the article on p.8 (October 1994) © Lands' End, Inc. All rights reserved; The Consumers' Association; Gruner + Jahr UK for the extracts from *Focus* magazine on p.17 (January 1994), p.19 (November 1993), p.75 (April 1993), p.94 (September 1994) and p.96 (April 1993); Harrington Kilbride Publishing Group plc for the article on p.31 (*Healthcare* Spring 1994); *The Independent* for the article on p.32 (from BBC serves up a celebrity ace for Grandstand viewers by David Lister 22.2.94); Richard Ehrlich for the article on p.34 (originally published in *She* magazine) © David Ehrlich; Phoenix Publishing and Media Limited for the article on pp.37-38 (*Essentially America* Summer 1994); David Higham Associates for the extract on p.43 (from *Mr Pye* by Mervin Peake 1975); Moorland Publishing Co. Ltd for the extract on p.49 (from *Visitor's Guide to Hampshire and the Isle of Wight* by John Barton 1990); Writers News Ltd for the article on p.58 (*Writing* Magazine Spring 1994); BBC Worldwide Publishing for the Go wild! extract on p.63 (*BBC Holidays* March 1994) and the article on p.89 (*BBC Vegetarian Good Food*); The Youth Hostels Association for the Win a Fabulous Holiday extract on p.64 (*Triangle* magazine Autumn 1993); John Boswell Associates for the extract on p.71 (from *The Complete Book of Long-distance and Competitive Cycling* by Tom Doughty, published by Simon and Schuster 1983); Julie Davidson for the article on pp.84-5 (*Infusion* magazine Spring 1994), printed with the kind permission of the Tea Council); Visual Imagination Ltd for the article by Judy Sloane on p.86 (*Film Review* No. 6); Reed Consumer Books Ltd for the extract on p.100 (from *New Ideas for Family Meals* by Louise Steele 1988).

Photographs: Tony Stone Images (p.9); London Stansted Airport (p.11); Bridgeman Art Library (p.34); Ace Photo Agency (p.37); Ronald Grant Archive (p.86).
Drawings by Leslie Marshall (pp.13, 65, 90).

Colour Paper 5 Section: Photographs by J. Pembrey (1A, 2A, 2C, 2D, 4E); ZEFA (1B, 2B, 1C, 1D, 3B, 4A, 4D); N. Luckhurst (2E: T-shirt, Shakespeare book, football strip, calendar, 4B); Mirror Syndication International (2E: kilt); The Image Bank (2E: pullover; Twinings tea); John Birdsall (2F, 2G, 2H, 2I); Ace Photo (3A, 4C); Tony Stone Worldwide (3C); Rex Features (3D). Drawings by Leslie Marshall (1E) and Shaun Williams (3E).

Book design by Peter Ducker MSTD

Practice Test 1

PAPER 1 READING (1 hour 15 minutes)

PART 1

*You are going to read a newspaper article about children's safety. Choose the most suitable heading from the list (**A–I**) for each part (**1–7**) of the article. There is one extra heading which you do not need to use. There is an example at the beginning (**0**).*
Mark your answers **on the separate answer sheet.**

A	Dangers off the road too
B	Trial period
C	Not what it appears to be
D	Dangerous driving
E	Dangers of fuel
F	First of many?
G	Learning to judge
H	Funds from industry
I	Danger in the city

Crash courses

0	*I*

It is a typical urban scene. Two cars are parked close together at the kerbside and a child is attempting to cross the road from between them. Down the street, another car looms. Houses flank the pavements and around the corner there is a brightly-lit petrol station.

1	

It is all extraordinarily realistic, but it is unreal. For the difference between this and thousands of similar locations throughout the country is that this street is indoors – it is a mock-up designed by studio set-builders from Anglia Television.

2	

We are standing inside a converted warehouse in Milton Keynes, home of a project which is the blueprint for an exciting new way of teaching children safety awareness, especially road safety. It is called Hazard Alley. If the centre proves successful and, having visited it, I am convinced it will, then its imaginative approach could easily be copied throughout the country.

3	

The project was started by the local authority in conjunction with the police. The finance came from commercial sponsorship by companies including Coca-Cola, Volkswagen and Anglia TV. There is already a catchy cartoon character mascot for the centre: Haza, the Hazard Alley cat.

4	

A novel setting for children to be taught and practise a wide range of safety topics, Hazard Alley takes its name from the dark alleyway in the centre of the converted warehouse which links the urban street scene and a series of country sets that focus on rural safety. As well as road drill, children are tutored in home safety and how to avoid trouble in playgrounds, parks, alleyways, near railways and on farmland.

5	

In the street scene, children practise the safe way to cross a road, including coping with parked vehicles, and are given a practical understanding of how long it takes a car to stop when travelling at 30 mph. Could the car they see looming down the road stop in time if a child stepped out between the parked cars? No, it would be through that wall at the end before it finished braking, 23 metres after the driver started to brake.

6	

On the mock-up petrol station forecourt, provided by Shell, the youngsters learn the dangers when filling a vehicle with petrol. They discuss car fires, the flammability of different components, why the car's engine must be switched off and why smoking and using a car phone are illegal on a garage forecourt.

7	

Hazard Alley is gearing up for its official opening, and the local schools which have experienced it so far have been testing out the centre before it launches into a full programme of group visits. It is already proving immensely popular. Eventually it may open to individual family groups. When that happens, it will be well worth a day trip: children will love it and they could learn something which may save their lives.

PART 2

*You are going to read a magazine article about being liked. For questions **8–15**, choose the answer (**A**, **B**, **C** or **D**) which you think fits best according to the text. Mark your answers **on the separate answer sheet**.*

LOVE ME DO!

I've just got to talk about this problem I'm having with my postman. It all began a year ago, after the birth of his first child. Not wanting to appear rude, I asked him about the baby. The next week, not wanting him to think I had asked out of mere politeness the week before, I asked all about the baby again. Now I can't break the habit. I freeze whenever I see him coming. The words 'How's the baby?' come out on their own. It's annoying. It holds me up. It holds him up. So why can't I stop it?

The answer, of course, is that I want him to like me. Come to think of it, I want everyone to like me. This was made clear to me the other day. I found myself in the bank, replying 'Oh, as it comes' when the cashier asked how I'd like the money. Even as she was handing me the £20 note, I realised I'd have no small change with which to buy my newspaper. But, not wanting her to dislike me (she'd already written '1 x £20' on the back of my cheque), said nothing.

In order to get the £20 note down to a decent, paper-buying size, I went into the grocer's. Not wanting to buy things I didn't actually need (I do have some pride, you know), I bought some large cans of beans and a frozen chicken for dinner that night. That got the price up to a respectable £5.12, which I duly paid. I then bought my paper at the station with my hard-gained £5 note.

With my sister, it wasn't the postman who was the problem, but the caretaker of her block of flats: 'All he ever does is moan and complain; he talks at me rather than to me, never listens to a word I say, and yet for some reason I'm always really nice to him. I'm worried in case I have a domestic crisis one day, and he won't lift a finger to help.'

I have a friend called Stephen, who is a prisoner of the call-waiting device he has had installed on his phone. 'I get this beeping sound to tell me there's another call on the line, but I can never bring myself to interrupt the person I'm talking to. So I end up not concentrating on what the first person's saying, while at the same time annoying the person who's trying to get through.'

What about at work? Richard Lawton, a management trainer, warns: 'Those managers who are actually liked by most of their staff are always those to whom being liked is not the primary goal. The qualities that make managers popular are being honest with staff, treating them as human beings and observing common courtesies like saying hello in the morning.' To illustrate the point, Richard cites the story of the company chairman who desperately wanted to be liked and who, after making one of his managers redundant, said with moist eyes that he was so, so sorry the man was leaving. To which the embittered employee replied: 'If you were that sorry, I wouldn't be leaving.' The lesson being, therefore, that if you try too hard to be liked, people won't like you.

The experts say it all starts in childhood. 'If children feel they can only get love from their parents by being good,' says Zelda West-Meads, a marriage guidance consultant, 'they develop low self-confidence and become compulsive givers.' But is there anything wrong in being a giver, the world not being exactly short of takers? Anne Cousins believes there is. 'There is a point at which giving becomes unhealthy,' she says. 'It comes when you do things for others but feel bad about it.'

I am now trying hard to say to people 'I feel uncomfortable about saying this, but ...', and tell myself 'Refusal of a request does not mean rejection of a person' and I find I can say almost anything to almost anyone.

8   Why does the writer ask the postman about his baby?
    A   He is interested in the baby.
    B   He wants to create a good impression.
    C   The postman is always polite to him.
    D   The postman enjoys a chat.

9   The writer went into the grocer's so that
    A   he had some food for dinner that night.
    B   he could buy a newspaper there.
    C   he could ask for £20 in change.
    D   he could buy something to get some change.

10   What do we find out about the writer's sister and the caretaker?
    A   She doesn't want to risk offending him.
    B   She doesn't pay attention to him.
    C   He refuses to help her.
    D   He asks her for advice.

11   How does Stephen feel about his call-waiting equipment?
    A   He gets annoyed when it interrupts him.
    B   He is unable to use it effectively.
    C   He finds it a relief from long conversations.
    D   He doesn't think it works properly.

12   Managers are more likely to be popular if they
    A   help staff with their problems.
    B   make sure the staff do not lose their jobs.
    C   encourage staff to be polite to each other.
    D   do not make too much effort to be liked.

13   When is it wrong to be 'a giver'?
    A   when it makes you ill
    B   when it does not give you pleasure
    C   when you make other people unhappy
    D   when you are unable to take from others

14   What do we learn from this article?
    A   If you tell the truth, it will not make people like you less.
    B   If you take time to talk to people, they will like you better.
    C   You should avoid unpleasant situations where possible.
    D   You shouldn't refuse other people's requests for help.

15   Why was this article written?
    A   to analyse the kinds of conversations people have
    B   to persuade people to be more polite to each other
    C   to encourage people to have more self-confidence
    D   to suggest ways of dealing with difficult people

*You are going to read a magazine article about a woman who goes gliding. Seven paragraphs have been removed from the article. Choose from the paragraphs (**A–H**) the one which fits each gap (**16–21**). There is one extra paragraph which you do not need to use. There is an example at the beginning (**0**).*
*Mark your answers **on the separate answer sheet**.*

IN PERSON

Twelve months ago, it was Lyn Ferguson who had the honour of cutting the ribbon to declare our Oakham Distribution Centre and offices open.

0	*H*

'I had my first glider flight when I was sixteen, but it wasn't until January 1986 that I took it up seriously. My boys had gone to school, I had lots of spare time and I thought, 'What am I going to do?' It just so happened that I had the opportunity to go up in a glider as a passenger to see if I liked it. I did.'

16	

'Really, it's very easy. All you need is coordination. The average person needs about 60 flights before they can go solo, completely alone, which sounds a lot, but the average instruction flight only takes around eight minutes, so training doesn't take long. I once did eleven trips in a day when I was training.'

17	

'Well, once you've done it alone, you can register with the British Gliding Association, then work towards your Bronze Badge. Each badge after that is about height, distance and endurance.

18	

Then, there are 10 km flights (straight out and back to the beginning), and 300 km flights, which show navigation skills. They're flown in a triangle starting and finishing at the airfield.'

19	

'Once, when I was in Australia, I lost height whilst attempting a 300 km flight and had to select a field to land in. Luckily, I spotted a field with a tractor in it and was able to land there. I think the farmer was pretty surprised when a glider suddenly landed next to him! He did let me use his phone, though.'

20	

'When you have a student who's finding things difficult, you convince them that they can do it. When they do, they're so pleased with themselves. When you land and they say "I can do it", it's brilliant.'

21	

'Flying is the main part, but there are other angles too. Gliding is like everything else. What you put in is what you get out. It's all about team work too. Everybody mucks in to push gliders around, pull cables in and generally help out. You can't do it on your own. I've met people in gliding from all walks of life, from lots of different countries, that I would never have met if I didn't go gliding.'

So, next time you see a glider soaring overhead, it may well be Lyn flying her way to another badge or, knowing her love of the sport, just gliding for the sheer fun of it.

A After eight years' gliding experience, Lyn has achieved her Bronze and Silver Badges and is an Assistant Rated Instructor. She hopes to go on and earn more badges, as well as becoming a Full Rated Instructor in the future. Her role as an instructor provides her with some of gliding's most rewarding moments.

B To those of us on the ground gazing up, the pilot's skills are there for all to see, as the glider soars effortlessly on the warm air thermals. Lyn is not one to boast about her training though.

C But for all the achievement of solo flight, glider pilots have to work for one another, and this is another side of gliding that Lyn enjoys and appreciates.

D So with the first solo flight behind you, what's next?

E Lyn thinks for a moment when she's asked if she's ever had any emergencies to contend with.

F As a result, a friend of hers flew in a glider alongside her along the Innsbruck Valley at mountain top height ... that's around seven thousand, four hundred feet.

G To get the Silver, for example, you have to get over 1,000 m in height, complete a five-hour flight and then a 50 km flight to a designated airfield.

H As PA to our Managing Director, Lyn has to be pretty level-headed, but in her spare time, she likes nothing better than to have her head in the clouds, indulging in her passion for gliding.

PART 4

You are going to read some information about airports in Britain. For questions
22–35, *choose from the airports* (**A–H**). *Some of the airports may be chosen more
than once. When more than one answer is required, these may be given in any
order. There is an example at the beginning* (**0**).
Mark your answers **on the separate answer sheet.**

Which airport:

does not sell anything to read?	**0**	*H*	
has shops which sell highly-priced goods?	**22**		**23**
seems to have put its seating in the wrong place?	**24**		
makes it very easy for passengers to find their way through?	**25**		
has its shops spread out?	**26**		
has a departure lounge which is not very impressive?	**27**		**28**
has a badly-situated café?	**29**		
changes its range of food according to the season?	**30**		
has an unexpectedly disappointing range of shops?	**31**		
has a good view of the planes?	**32**		
has facilities for people who are travelling for work?	**33**		**34**
needs modernising?	**35**		

Which airport?

The choice of where to fly from has never been greater, particularly for those flying on a package holiday. For each airport, we looked at the facilities (e.g. restaurants, waiting areas, etc.) offered before going through passport control (land-side) and after going through passport control (air-side).

A   Heathrow 4

The check-in hall is spacious and modern. There are few land-side shops but the essentials are available. A café with pine seating and a medium range of hot dishes and salads is situated upstairs. There are more facilities air-side. The shops are clustered into the central part of the 500-metre long hall, and expensive ranges are well represented. There's plenty of natural light from the windows that overlook the runway and lots of seating away from the shopping area.

B   Manchester 2

The check-in hall has a high glass roof which lets in natural light. The café is at one end and slightly separated from the rest of the facilities, which makes it much more pleasant. There's also an up-market coffee shop. Hundreds of seats – little used when we visited despite the passengers crowded below – are available upstairs. The departure lounge is bright and has plenty of space, the cafeteria is pleasant.

C   Stansted

Passengers can walk in a straight line from the entrance, through the check-in to the monorail that takes them to their plane. Land-side, ⟫→

there's a cluster of fast food outlets that sell baked potatoes, American burgers and filled rolls. All seating is in the same area away from the check-in and shops. There's a surprisingly small number of shops considering Stansted's claims to be a major London airport, although basic stores like a chemist and bookshop are here. The large departure lounge has blue seats and grey carpet. There's a large tax-free and luxury goods shopping area and a café.

D Heathrow 2

Avoid travelling from here if you can. The check-in area is unpleasant with a claustrophobic low roof and scores of pillars. The upstairs café is noisy because it is next to the music shop. The departure lounge is also too small with illuminated advertisements hanging from its low ceiling.

E Manchester 1

The large, low check-in hall is the least impressive part of the terminal. Beyond that is a pleasant shopping mall with a wide range of shops and snack bars. The self-service eating area has a good range of foods from steak and chips to salads. There is also a more formal restaurant mostly used for business lunches. The departure lounge is large and bright.

F Edinburgh

The eating options range from a coffee shop to a self-service restaurant, and a reasonable variety of shops are scattered around the land-side area rather than being collected in one area. The air-side food arrangements are mainly limited to rolls and buns.

G East Midlands

The check-in area is in a long, low building where the roof is supported by a forest of pillars which interrupt the line of vision. There's a café and bar upstairs along with a pizza restaurant during the summer. The main eating area is downstairs and mainly serves sandwiches and cakes along with a hot dish of the day. The departure lounge is pleasant with natural light and plenty of dark blue seats. The Sherwood Lounge has easy chairs and sofas and is aimed at commercial travellers.

H Cardiff

The facilities are simple and the decoration is showing its age. Shopping is extremely limited with only bare essentials available. There are no books or magazines for sale. The restaurant is unappealing. The tiny departure lounge is dark and uninviting.

PAPER 2 WRITING (1 hour 30 minutes)

PART 1

*You **must** answer this question.*

1 You are interested in attending a language course in England next summer.
You have seen the advertisement below. You have also talked to your English
teacher and she has suggested some things that you should check before
you register.

Read the advertisement below, together with your teacher's note. Then write
to the language school, asking for information about the points mentioned by
your teacher, and anything else that you think is important.

SUMMER LANGUAGE COURSES

2 weeks, 3 weeks, 1 month

Beautiful English market town. Full sports
and social programme. Accommodation
with friendly English families. Helpful
teachers. Small classes.

Full details from: Ian Lawrence,
The Smart School of English, High Street,
Little Bonnington

It's a great idea for you to
do a language course in
England. Be careful to choose
a good school. When you
write, ask about these things:
– student numbers, ages
– details of sports programme
  etc.
– local facilities
– teachers' qualifications
Let me know if you need any
more help. Good luck!

Write a **letter** of between **120–180** words in an appropriate style on the next
page. Do not write any addresses.

PART 1

....

....

....

....

....

....

....

....

....

....

....

....

....

....

....

....

....

....

....

....

....

....

....

....

....

....

....

....

PART 2

Write an answer to **one** *of the questions* **2–5** *in this part. Write your answer in* **120–180** *words in an appropriate style on the next page, putting the question number in the box.*

2   An international young people's magazine is investigating the question:
    Do young people today really know what they want from life?

    Write a short **article** for this magazine on this topic based on your own experience.

3   You have decided to enter this competition.

> ## Exciting chance for writers!
>
> Write a short story and win a Great Prize
>
> Your entry must begin or end with the following words:
>
> *No matter what people said about Alex, I knew he was a true friend.*

Write your **story** for the competition.

4   You are attending a summer language course and have been asked to report on a local leisure facility (e.g. cinema, sports hall, etc.) for the benefit of students attending the next course.

    Write your **report** describing the facility and what it has to offer, and commenting on its good and bad points.

5   **Background reading texts**

    Answer **one** of the following two questions based on your reading of **one** of the set books (see p. v). Write the title of the book next to the question number box.

    Either   **(a)** Describe your favourite character in the book and explain what you like about him/her.

    or   **(b)** Explain how the physical setting of the book is important to the success of the story.

PART 2

Question	

....

....

....

....

....

....

....

....

....

....

....

....

....

....

....

....

....

....

....

....

....

....

....

....

....

....

....

....

PAPER 3   USE OF ENGLISH (1 hour 15 minutes)

PART 1

For questions **1–15***, read the text below and decide which answer* **A, B, C** *or* **D**
best fits each space. There is an example at the beginning **(0)***.*
Mark your answers **on the separate answer sheet.**

Example:

0   **A** expect   **B** count   **C** claim   **D** prepare

0	A	B	C	D
	▬	▭	▭	▭

ACTION SCENES IN FILMS

Modern cinema audiences **(0)** .... to see plenty of thrilling scenes in action films. These scenes, which are **(1)** .... as stunts, are usually **(2)** .... by stuntmen who are specially trained to do dangerous things safely. **(3)** .... can crash a car, but if you're shooting a film, you have to be extremely **(4)** .... , sometimes stopping **(5)** .... in front of the camera and film crew. At an early **(6)** .... in the production, an expert stuntman is **(7)** .... in to work out the action scenes and form a team. He is the only person who can go **(8)** .... the wishes of the director, **(9)** .... he will usually only do this in the **(10)** .... of safety.

Many famous actors like to do the dangerous parts themselves, which produces better shots, since stuntmen don't have to **(11)** .... in for the actors. Actors like to become **(12)** .... in all the important aspects of the character they are playing, but without the recent progress in safety equipment, insurance companies would never **(13)** .... them take the risk. To do their own stunts, actors need to be good athletes, but they must also be sensible and know their **(14)** .... . If they were to be hurt, the film would **(15)** .... to a sudden halt.

1 **A** remarked   **B** known   **C** referred   **D** named

.2 **A** performed   **B** given   **C** fulfilled   **D** displayed

3 **A** Everyone   **B** Someone   **C** Anyone   **D** No-one

4 **A** detailed   **B** plain   **C** straight   **D** precise

5 **A** right   **B** exact   **C** direct   **D** strict

6 **A** period   **B** minute   **C** part   **D** stage

7 **A** led   **B** taken   **C** drawn   **D** called

8 **A** over   **B** against   **C** through   **D** across

9 **A** despite   **B** so   **C** although   **D** otherwise

10 **A** interests   **B** needs   **C** purposes   **D** regards

11 **A** work   **B** get   **C** put   **D** stand

12 **A** connected   **B** arranged   **C** involved   **D** affected

13 **A** allow   **B** let   **C** permit   **D** admit

14 **A** limits   **B** ends   **C** frontiers   **D** borders

15 **A** come   **B** fall   **C** pull   **D** go

PART 2

*For questions **16–30**, read the text below and think of the word which best fits each space. Use only **one** word in each space. There is an example at the beginning (**0**).*
*Write your word **on the separate answer sheet**.*

Example: | 0 | *or* | | 0 | __ __ __ |

SHARKS

For anyone who wants either to film **(0)** .... study great white sharks, Australian expert, Rodney Fox, is the first contact. Fox knows exactly **(16)** .... the sharks will be at different times of the year; and can even predict **(17)** .... they will behave around blood, divers and other sharks. He understands them as well as **(18)** .... else alive. In fact, he's lucky to *be* alive; a 'great white' once **(19)** .... to bite him in half.

Three decades **(20)** .... this near-fatal attack, Fox still carries the physical scars, but feels **(21)** .... hate for his attacker. Instead he organises three or four trips **(22)** .... year to bring scientists and photographers to the kingdom of the great white shark. **(23)** .... main aim of these trips is to improve people's understanding of an animal **(24)** .... evil reputation has become an excuse for killing it.

Great white sharks are not as amusing as dolphins and seals, **(25)** .... their role in the ocean is critical. They kill off sick animals, helping to prevent the spread **(26)** .... disease and to maintain the balance in the ocean's food chains. Fox feels a responsibility to act **(27)** .... a guardian of great white sharks. **(28)** .... the scientists, film makers and photographers can communicate their sense of wonder **(29)** .... other people, he is confident that understanding **(30)** .... replace hatred.

PART 3

*For questions **31–40**, complete the second sentence so that it has a similar meaning to the first sentence, using the word given. **Do not change the word given**. You must use between two and five words, including the word given. There is an example at the beginning (**0**).*
*Write **only** the missing words **on the separate answer sheet**.*

Example:

0   I last saw him at my 21st birthday party.
       since

       I .... my 21st birthday party.

The gap can be filled by the words 'haven't seen him since' so you write:

0	*haven't seen him since*	**0**	**0** **1** **2**

---

31   'You've broken my radio, Frank!' said Jane.
        accused

        Jane .... her radio.

32   My car really needs to be repaired soon.
        must

        I really .... repaired soon.

33   Susan regrets not buying that house.
        wishes

        Susan .... that house.

34   I could never have succeeded without your help.
        you

        I could never have succeeded .... me.

35   I thought I might run out of cash, so I took my cheque-book with me.
        case

        I took my cheque-book with me .... out of cash.

36 Linda's plans for a picnic have been spoilt by the weather.
fallen

Linda's plans for a picnic .... because of the weather.

37 The bread was too stale to eat.
fresh

The bread .... to eat.

38 Perhaps Brian went home early.
may

Brian .... home early.

39 I can't possibly work in all this noise!
impossible

It .... work in all this noise!

40 The thief suddenly realised that the police were watching him.
watched

The thief suddenly realised that he .... by the police.

PART 4

*For questions **41–55**, read the text below and look carefully at each line. Some of the lines are correct, and some have a word which should not be there. If a line is correct, put a tick (✓) by the number **on the separate answer sheet**. If a line has a word which should **not** be there, write the word **on the separate answer sheet**. There are two examples at the beginning (**0** and **00**).*

Examples:

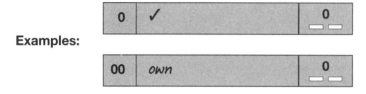

WHY I DISLIKE COMPUTERS

0	Almost everyone says that computers are wonderful and that they are
00	changing our own lives for the better by making everything faster and
41	more reliable, but I'm not so much sure that this is the case.
42	The other day I was standing in a large department store until
43	waiting to pay for a couple of films for my camera when the assistant
44	announced that the computer which controlled the till it had stopped
45	working. I didn't think this was a big problem and I set myself off to
46	find another counter, but of course, all the machines are one part of
47	the same system. So there we were: a shop full of customers, money
48	at the ready, waiting to make our purchases, but it was quite clear that
49	none out of the assistants knew what to do. They weren't allowed to
50	take our money and give to customers a written receipt, because the
51	sales wouldn't then have been recorded on the computer system.
52	In the end, like with many other people, I left my shopping on the
53	counter and walked out. Don't you think so that's ridiculous? It would
54	never have happened before computers, and that, for me, is all the
55	problem: we are beginning to depend on these machines for so
	completely that we simply can't manage without them any more.

PART 5

*For questions **56–65**, read the text below. Use the word given in capitals at the end of each line to form a word that fits in the space in the same line. There is an example at the beginning **(0)**. Write your word **on the separate answer sheet**.*

Example:

0	*unusual*	0

CAMERON PARK

At first light, there is nothing **(0)** .... about the town of Cameron Park in California but, as the day begins and the town comes to **(56)** .... , you can't help **(57)** .... that, among the cars, there are light aeroplanes moving along the roads towards the airport.

USUAL
LIVE
NOTICE

When the town was **(58)** .... built, a small airport was included for the **(59)** .... of people flying in to look at the properties which were for **(60)** .... , but it soon became clear to the developers that this was an attraction in itself. The streets were **(61)** .... so that planes could use them, the mailboxes near the road were made **(62)** .... to avoid passing wings, and all the electricity cables were buried **(63)** .... .

ORIGIN
CONVENIENT
SELL
WIDE
SHORT
GROUND

Now, there is every **(64)** .... that the residents will have a private plane in their garage and use it with the same **(65)** .... other people enjoy with their cars.

LIKELY
FREE

PAPER 4   LISTENING (approximately 40 minutes)

PART 1

You will hear people talking in eight different situations.
For questions 1–8, choose the best answer A, B or C.

1   You are visiting a museum when you hear this man addressing a group of people.
   Who is he?

   A   a security guard

   B   a tourist guide

   C   a museum guide

	1

2   You're in a restaurant when you overhear one of the waiters talking.
   Who is he talking about?

   A   a colleague

   B   the manager

   C   a customer

	2

3   You're waiting in a hospital corridor when you hear this woman talking.
   What does she say about her doctor?

   A   He's made a mistake.

   B   He's been unhelpful.

   C   He's been untruthful.

	3

4   You are out shopping when you hear a shop assistant talking to a customer.
   What is she refusing to do?

   A   give him some money

   B   change a faulty item

   C   repair something

	4

5   Listen to this woman introducing the next speaker at a conference.
Why has she been asked to introduce him?

   A   He is an old friend.

   B   He is a former student of hers.

   C   He is a colleague.

	5

6   You are staying in a farmhouse when you hear your host on the telephone.
Who is he talking to?

   A   a supplier

   B   a customer

   C   an employee

	6

7   You hear this critic talking on the radio.
What is she recommending?

   A   a film

   B   a book

   C   an exhibition

	7

8   You are walking up the street when you hear this man talking to a woman at her front door.
What does he want to do?

   A   interview her

   B   help her

   C   advise her

	8

PART 2

You will hear a student called Bill talking about his holiday job.
*For questions **9–18**, complete the notes which summarise what he says. You will need to write a word or a short phrase in the box.*

Reason for doing job:

	9

Building used to be a

	10

Good position because it's near

	11

Main alteration: owner has added

	12

Bill's favourite task:

	13

Owner is very careful about

	14

Attitude of male residents to staff:

	15

Problem with woman who
thought he was

	16

Other staff treated Bill as

	17

Bill is going back in order to

	18

PART 3

You will hear five different women talking about parties.
*For questions **19–23**, choose from the list **A–F** what they describe. Use the letters only once. There is one extra letter which you do not need to use.*

A   She regretted having gone.

B   She was surprised she enjoyed it.

Speaker 1		19
Speaker 2		20
Speaker 3		21
Speaker 4		22
Speaker 5		23

C   She was embarrassed by her friends.

D   She thought it was badly organised.

E   She hadn't known what sort of event it was.

F   She met someone who admired her.

PART 4

You will hear a conversation between two teenagers, Nick and Sandra.
For questions 24–30, decide which statements are true or false and mark your
answers **T** *for True or* **F** *for False.*

24   Sandra had to do some housework before coming out.　　　　　　 24

25   Sandra envies Nick.　　　　　　 25

26   Sandra is angry with her mother.　　　　　　 26

27   Sandra has failed her exams.　　　　　　 27

28   Nick sympathises with Sandra's mother.　　　　　　 28

29   Sandra has lost the tickets.　　　　　　 29

30   Nick will go to the next concert on his own.　　　　　　 30

PAPER 5 SPEAKING (14 minutes)

Part 1

You tell the examiner about yourself. The examiner may ask you questions such as: Where are you from? How do you usually spend your free time? What are your plans for the future? Your partner does the same.

Part 2

The examiner gives you two pictures to look at and asks you to talk about them for about a minute. Your partner does the same with two different pictures.

Part 3

The examiner gives you a photograph or drawing to look at with your partner. You are asked to solve a problem or come to a decision about something in the picture. For example, you might be asked to decide the best way to use some rooms in a language school. You discuss the problem together.

Part 4

You are asked more questions connected with your discussion in Part 3. For example, you might be asked to talk about the best ways of studying.

Practice Test 2

PAPER 1   READING (1 hour 15 minutes)

PART 1

You are going to read a magazine article about exercising in water. Choose from the list (A–I) the sentence which best summarises each part (1–7) of the article. There is one extra sentence which you do not need to use. There is an example at the beginning (0).
Mark your answers on the separate answer sheet.

A	You are unlikely to cause yourself an injury in water.
B	It is not as easy as it looks.
C	Aqua fitness can do more than simply help heal injuries.
D	You can lose weight and enjoy yourself at the same time.
E	You can strengthen your heart and muscles by training every day.
F	Your body will adapt to exercising in water.
G	Don't worry about what you look like.
H	Exercise in water puts less pressure on the heart.
I	The idea of exercising in water is not new.

Making a SPLASH

0	*I*

The last thing many people expect to do in a swimming pool these days is swim. The latest fitness phenomenon to make a big splash at the local pool is aqua fitness. The properties of water have long been known to make it one of the safest and most effective media in which to exercise. Physiotherapists have used it for years and, even as far back as the Romans, the value of water for healing has been recognised.

1	

Today 'aqua fitness', as it is known, has seen exercising in the swimming pool progressing from merely being an activity for the recovery of an injury. Aqua fitness has become a valuable training aid even for professional athletes who use it to reduce the risk of overtraining. However, that's not to say that exercising in water isn't ideal for the rest of us too, from the young to the old, from the fit to those who do suffer from complaints such as arthritis.

2	

Exercising in water raises the heart rate less than land

aerobics. Lydia Campbell, a fitness expert, says there are no conclusive studies on why it has a less drastic effect on your heart, but there are some factors that partly explain it. Lydia says, 'Water is supportive, as we all know, and with blood flowing more easily, there is less stress on the heart.'

3	

There are other benefits to working out in water such as the fact that your muscles are less likely to ache the following day, the water has a massaging effect on the body, and of course, there is always the possibility of getting a bit slimmer. It is generally thought that an aqua fitness workout can use from 450 to 700 calories an hour. And don't forget, water is fun – exercising to music in water is a unique experience!

4	

The reassuring element of exercising in water is that, apart from doing you good, it is relatively difficult to do anything that is going to harm you.

5	

As far as modesty is concerned, if you miss a step,

carry a little more excess weight than you feel comfortable with or just feel embarrassed because you haven't exercised before, there is no need to be anxious as everything is hidden beneath the water level!

6	

Getting used to moving in water takes a little time because of the gravity changes on the body. Running in water will be easier if your body has lots of muscle, but don't worry about this not being the case, as the exercising in water will strengthen muscles anyway. Soon you will be able to move more strongly through the pool.

7	

Classes usually start with a warm-up aimed at stimulating and raising the body temperature. Using the properties of water in an aqua workout can create an effective training programme that might change some previous ideas about how easy exercising in water is. Try running in shallow knee-deep water. It's easy, but try running in thigh-deep water and things suddenly get more difficult – chest-deep water is even harder, as the water resistance increases.

PART 2

You are going to read a newspaper article about a television presenter called Sue Barker. For questions 8–15, choose the answer (A, B, C or D) which you think fits best according to the text.

Mark your answers on the separate answer sheet.

SUE BARKER, the former tennis star, is to present the BBC TV Sports Programme *Grandstand* this summer. The BBC will shortly announce her promotion to one of television's top sports posts, confirming a rise in the media ranks that has been almost as rapid as her progress up the ladder of international tennis in the 1970s.

It is a remarkable comeback to national fame for a woman originally known for being the girlfriend of a pop star and for being a British player who won the French Open tennis tournament.

Her new media career is already very successful. It had a sudden beginning. A succession of injuries and a fall in her ranking from 16th to 63rd caused her to announce her retirement from the game in a dramatic on-court speech at the Australian Open tournament in 1984.

'I took the car back to my hotel where a message was waiting for me to ring a TV station in Sydney. I thought, "Oh God, not another interview", but they asked me to come and start on their sports programme the next day to give expert comment. There was no training, nothing.'

There was no training either when David Hill, then head of sport on Sky TV, recruited her two years ago to be one of the presenters on its Saturday sports programme.

'I turned up and was told my first broadcast was in a few minutes' time. It was a classic, absolutely awful. I rattled through it, it wasn't even making sense, and then I was left for the last four seconds just smiling at the camera.

'It was the longest four seconds of my life. Afterwards I said I wanted to give up, but David said, "You've only made two mistakes, I never sack anyone until they've made three". So I carried on doing five-minute slots – the sports news round-ups – which proved to be very good on-the-job training. Then came the approach from the BBC.'

While Sky took a quiet pride in the fact that the BBC wanted to sign up its star, its annoyance at losing Barker was understandable. It had allowed the BBC to have her for the tennis season and offered a half-and-half arrangement when the BBC wanted to sign her full-time – but the BBC was not interested. Sam Chisholm, Sky's chief executive, decided to take legal action.

In the BBC's tennis team, the strengths of Sue Barker were immediately obvious. She offered a number of technical insights, not just into the game but into the players' mental state, and was not afraid to be critical of those on the court who are still friends, a rare quality among the large number of former sports stars that fill the BBC commentary boxes.

For Barker, being a critic was not always easy, especially as she mixed socially with the players. They did sometimes get upset about it. 'Martina Navratilova watches everything, absolutely everything, and she came up to me quite angry one day, saying "I heard you, I heard what you said about Steffi Graf". But I will tell them exactly why I thought they weren't playing well, compare their performance with a previous one and, if they can honestly say to me they did play well, then I will apologise.'

Having been angry at some of the criticism of *her* during her 13 years of playing international tennis, she feels she can turn that knowledge to good use. 'I know what hurts and what doesn't hurt, and athletes tend to trust other athletes.'

8   What does the writer say about Sue Barker's career?
    A   She took a long time to become famous as a tennis star.
    B   She is better known as a TV presenter than a tennis star.
    C   She obtained an important TV job after a short time.
    D   She has tried a career in pop music.

9   What does 'it' in line 10 refer to?
    A   her tennis career
    B   her comeback
    C   her success on TV
    D   her fame

10   She became a sports commentator because
    A   she was advised to do so by tennis experts.
    B   an Australian TV channel suggested it.
    C   she decided she would prefer it to tennis.
    D   she was tired of being interviewed by other people.

11   What happened when she presented a Saturday sports programme?
    A   She made a better impression than she expected.
    B   The TV company liked the way she smiled at the camera.
    C   She talked for too long and too fast.
    D   The boss wasn't sure whether to sack her or not.

12   How did Sky TV feel when the BBC employed her?
    A   They turned down the offer to share her.
    B   They were glad for her sake.
    C   They did not want to lose her.
    D   They had expected this to happen.

13   How is she different from other sports commentators?
    A   She still has a lot of friends in the game.
    B   She has very good technical background.
    C   She finds it difficult to praise the players.
    D   She speaks the truth about friends.

14   What does she feel she can offer as a sports commentator?
    A   She can give athletes advice on dealing with the camera.
    B   She can make comments which athletes accept.
    C   She can help athletes to get on with each other.
    D   She can attract new viewers to sports programmes.

15   This article was written about Sue Barker because
    A   she is going to be in the public view a lot.
    B   there is a court case between Sky TV and the BBC.
    C   she has recently given up tennis.
    D   a well-known tennis star was recently upset by her.

*You are going to read a newspaper article about an artist. Seven paragraphs have been removed from the article. Choose from the paragraphs (**A–H**) the one which fits each gap (**16–21**). There is one extra paragraph which you do not need to use. There is an example at the beginning (**0**).*

*Mark your answers **on the separate answer sheet**.*

The life of Georgia O'Keeffe

Georgia O'Keeffe was born in 1887 and grew up in Sun Prairie, Wisconsin, a farming town settled only 40 years earlier.

0	*H*

When she was 16, her family moved to Virginia, and O'Keeffe studied art at the Art Institute of Chicago. At 23, she had a crisis of confidence and spoke of giving up painting, but over the next two years she taught art in Texas and in South Carolina, and eventually regained her desire to paint.

16	

O'Keeffe lived and studied in New York on and off for three years, taking time off to teach in Virginia, South Carolina and again in Texas. Always independent-minded, in Texas she became known for her strange clothes.

17	

A friend showed O'Keeffe's drawings to Alfred Stieglitz, the greatest photographer in America and owner of the forward-looking 291 Gallery in New York. When he unwrapped O'Keeffe's charcoal drawings,

he was amazed. 'I realised that I had never seen anything like it before.'

18	

A year later, O'Keeffe gave up her teaching and started painting full-time in Manhattan, Maine and at the Stieglitz family home in Lake George, New York. She also joined Stieglitz's circle of friends, which included some of the most important writers, painters and photographers in America.

19	

While her work grew in confidence, her life with Stieglitz was full of difficulties. He encouraged her work but wanted her to be an obedient wife. In his role as her dealer he sought dictatorial control over the sale and exhibition of her work. O'Keeffe felt imprisoned by her marriage, genuinely loving though it was.

20

And it gave rise to some of her greatest paintings: landscapes, studies of architecture, and still-lifes. In still-life she became obsessed with the animal skeletons she had collected in the desert.

21

When Georgia O'Keeffe died, she was a year short of her century. Relatives gave some of O'Keeffe's work to American museums. They show the courage and persistence of one of the most remarkable of all women painters.

A During this period, O'Keeffe made a series of charcoal studies which she called her 'Special' drawings. These were the first work of her artistic maturity. And they were to lead to her first great romantic involvement.

B After Stieglitz died, O'Keeffe rarely visited the East Coast, and the life she led in New Mexico was increasingly solitary. She continued to work, though with decreasing energy (she was now 60 years old). Her work grew steadily in value and she became a very rich woman.

C Stieglitz exhibited the drawings without O'Keeffe's knowledge. Though initially outraged, she knew that 291 was the best possible venue for her work – and Stieglitz himself the best possible dealer. With time, he became equally passionate about O'Keeffe herself. She was 30 and Stieglitz was 53. In 1924 they married.

D She found her escape in New Mexico. She had long preferred the empty landscapes of the American West to the greenery of the East Coast. Even though she remained devoted to the ageing Stieglitz and spent winters with him in New York, New Mexico was her home for the rest of her life.

E The role did not entirely suit her. Solitary by nature and the only woman artist in a group of opinionated men, she was very aware of the oppression of women. Some of the men resented her, feeling threatened by a woman of such exceptional talent.

F O'Keeffe denied the connection and late in life she abruptly finished an interview when asked about it. She also painted New York's cityscape as well as rural architecture.

G O'Keeffe did not feel that her future lay in teaching, but then as now there were few other ways for an artist to earn a living. So she decided to take a teaching degree in New York, and her life was changed forever.

H O'Keeffe was drawn towards art from an early age. She was brilliant at drawing and, at 13, told a friend, 'I'm going to be an artist'.

PART 4

You are going to read a magazine article about New York cafés. For questions 22–34, choose from the cafés (A–H). Some of the cafés may be chosen more than once. When more than one answer is required, these may be given in any order. There is an example at the beginning (0).

For question 35, choose the answer (A, B, C or D) which you think fits best according to the text.

Mark your answers on the separate answer sheet.

Which of the cafés:

is close to a theatre?	**0**	*H*
does not have very interesting food?	**22**	
is near a well-known monument?	**23**	
is floating?	**24**	
offers some dishes for the health-conscious?	**25**	
is good for sitting and watching others?	**26**	**27**
appeals particularly to tourists?	**28**	
may offer you the chance of some physical exercise?	**29**	
is known by few people?	**30**	
is fairly cheap?	**31**	
has exciting American food?	**32**	
is good for a special evening out?	**33**	**34**

35 The purpose of the text is to

    A identify the liveliest outdoor café in New York.

    B identify the outdoor café in New York with the best food.

    C offer information about a range of eating opportunities in New York.

    D offer information about the eating habits of people in New York.

Big Apple al fresco

Scattered throughout the city of New York are dozens of 'secret' gardens, quiet corners, terraces and rooftops where you can escape the urban rush and dine amidst trees and flowering plants.

A   TAVERN ON THE GREEN

Some call it a tourist trap, but the architecture and woodland setting guarantee a long and healthy life for this Central Park restaurant. Dinner in the garden on a summer's night, wrapped in the scent of a thousand flowers and lit by Japanese lanterns, is truly an affair to remember. And the extravagant desserts are a luscious way to celebrate a birthday or other special occasion.

B   BOATHOUSE CAFÉ

While tourists are queuing up for tables at Tavern on the Green, New Yorkers head deeper into Central Park for lunch at this charming, relatively inexpensive café. The main attraction here is the setting, which overlooks the park's Boathouse Pond with the skyscrapers of midtown in the ⟫→

background. The food at the Boathouse is admittedly unimpressive although you won't go wrong with the pasta dishes or burgers.

C COURTYARD CAFÉ & BAR

Located in the heart of midtown near Grand Central Terminal, this eatery in the Doral Court Hotel qualifies as one of New York's best-kept secrets. The garden here, though small, is one of the city's finest with umbrella-shaded tables next to a sparkling waterfall.

D AMERICAN FESTIVAL CAFÉ

'Golden Boy', the famous statue, oversees the festivities at this restaurant situated in the shadow of New York's Art Deco architectural masterpiece. In winter, the outdoor section of the café is transformed into the Rockefeller Center Skating Rink; in summer, the shaded, linen-draped tables make an inviting prospect after a hard morning of shopping.

E RIVER CAFÉ

New York City's best outdoor dining experience is across the Brooklyn Bridge at this boat-restaurant moored in the East River. In an informal survey, six out of seven New Yorkers picked the River Café as the best place in the city to propose marriage. Positive features: stunning views of the Manhattan skyline, and of picture-perfect sunsets; inventive contemporary cooking with an American accent.

F MANHATTAN CHILLI COMPANY

Outdoor cafés are thick on the ground in Greenwich Village — it's hardly worth recommending one, since visitors so quickly find their own. It's easy to walk by the Manhattan Chilli Company which looks like just another quaint Village restaurant from the street. Step inside, though, and you'll discover gigantic bowls of good chilli served in a peaceful garden.

G YAFFA CAFÉ

When the western half of Greenwich Village changed into a center for tourists, the area's artists and musicians moved east to the neighbourhood known as Alphabet City. For a glimpse of arty New York, 1990s style, take a seat in Yaffa's uniquely urban garden; order a plate of food and a pot of herb tea and watch the world go by.

H JOSEPHINA

An excellent position across the street from Lincoln Center for the Performing Arts draws diners to this exotic restaurant; the delicately seasoned recipes and fresher-than-fresh ingredients bring them back. Owner/chef Louis Lanza uses flavoured oils and fresh stocks to delight the taste-buds without excessive sugar or fat. (The exception: sinfully rich desserts. Shrugs Lanza, 'Nobody's perfect.') Josephina offers two outdoor options, a sidewalk café that's perfect for people-watching and a lushly landscaped back garden.

PAPER 2 WRITING (1 hour 30 minutes)

PART 1

*You **must** answer this question.*

1 Your friend has seen this job advertisement and is planning to apply. You worked for the same company last year. Using the information in the advertisement and the notes you have made on it, tell your friend what the job was really like and give him or her any advice you think necessary.

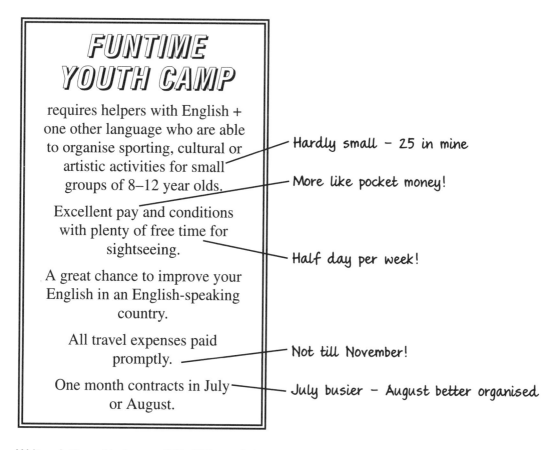

Write a **letter** of between **120–180** words in an appropriate style on the next page. Do not write any addresses.

PART 1

....
....
....
....
....
....
....
....
....
....
....
....
....
....
....
....
....
....
....
....
....
....
....
....
....
....
....
....
....

PART 2

Write an answer to **one** *of the questions* **2–5** *in this part. Write your answer in* **120–180** *words in an appropriate style on the next page, putting the question number in the box.*

2   Your school magazine or company newsletter has decided to use its back page for a regular entertainment section. Write a **review** of a film or play you have seen recently, describing the film or play and saying why you would or would not recommend others to go and see it.

3   You see this notice in a magazine for learners of English, and decide to send in a story:

> We wish to publish a collection of stories from our readers, all with the title **The day that did most for my English**.
>
>   If you have an interesting or amusing story which you would like to share with others, please send it to us as soon as possible.

Write your **story** for the magazine.

4   Your teacher has asked you to describe some of the ways in which the place where you live has changed during your lifetime. Write a **description**, explaining whether these changes are for the better or the worse, and why you think this.

5   **Background reading texts**

Answer **one** of the following two questions based on your reading of **one** of the set books (see p. v). Write the title of the book next to the question number box.

Either   **(a)** Describe any character or event in the book which you find improbable and explain why.

or   **(b)** Describe the opening of the book and say whether it made you want to read the rest of the story. Explain why or why not.

PART 2

Question	

....

....

....

....

....

....

....

....

....

....

....

....

....

....

....

....

....

....

....

....

....

....

....

....

....

....

....

....

....

PAPER 3   USE OF ENGLISH (1 hour 15 minutes)

PART 1

*For questions **1–15**, read the text below and decide which answer **A, B, C** or **D** best fits each space. There is an example at the beginning (**0**).*
*Mark your answers **on the separate answer sheet**.*

Example:
0   A in   **B** along   **C** up   **D** over

0	A	B	C	D
	▬	▭	▭	▭

A VISITOR FOR MISS DREDGER

Every summer Miss Dredger took (**0**) .... visitors at Clôs de Joi. It was a square house with a (**1**) .... across the island to the sea, with the island of Jersey on the (**2**) .... .

Miss Dredger had (**3**) .... a carriage to take her down the harbour hill. (**4**) .... it was a steep descent, she would (**5**) .... have taken it in her purposeful stride, and would even have returned (**6**) .... foot up the long slope, for Miss Dredger scorned all physical (**7**) .... .

Nevertheless, she had (**8**) .... on a carriage this (**9**) .... morning, for she had a gentleman to meet at the harbour. Both he and his luggage must be got up the harbour hill. It was (**10**) .... that the luggage could not walk up on its own and from what she knew about men, it was ten (**11**) .... one that her new lodger (**12**) .... be as helpless as his luggage.

And so, as the carriage had to go down the hill before it could come up again, Miss Dredger, with her sharp (**13**) .... of logic, decided that, in order to (**14**) .... use of this fact, it would be as well to be (**15**) .... for at Clôs de Joi.

1   **A** sight   **B** vision   **C** view   **D** look

2   **A** distance   **B** background   **C** outskirts   **D** horizon

3   **A** ordered   **B** required   **C** commanded   **D** asked

4   **A** However   **B** Although   **C** Despite   **D** Even

5   **A** commonly   **B** actually   **C** mostly   **D** normally

6   **A** at   **B** on   **C** with   **D** off

7   **A** weakness   **B** lightness   **C** tenderness   **D** softness

8   **A** decided   **B** chosen   **C** arranged   **D** considered

9   **A** definite   **B** certain   **C** particular   **D** individual

10 **A** honest   **B** simple   **C** direct   **D** plain

11 **A** to   **B** by   **C** for   **D** under

12 **A** should   **B** would   **C** ought   **D** could

13 **A** sense   **B** idea   **C** feeling   **D** impression

14 **A** take   **B** have   **C** make   **D** get

15 **A** looked   **B** visited   **C** sent   **D** called

PART 2

*For questions **16–30**, read the text below and think of the word which best fits each space. Use only **one** word in each space. There is an example at the beginning (**0**).*
*Write your word **on the separate answer sheet**.*

Example: | 0 | *one* | 0 |

THE HORSE IN ART

There is little doubt that **(0)** .... of the chief roles of the horse in art, just **(16)** .... in life, is that of our servant and companion. We can have very little idea of **(17)** .... a horse feels in its natural state. Left to itself, **(18)** .... is unlikely that it would pull a plough, take a soldier **(19)** .... a dangerous situation in battle, **(20)** .... do most of the other things that have attracted painters and writers to the animal ever **(21)** .... the dawn of history.

The horse is controlled **(22)** .... the wishes of its owner. When we describe it, we say it has **(23)** .... virtues and qualities we most admire in ourselves and it is as the symbol **(24)** .... these qualities that it has so often **(25)** .... praised by painters and poets. Then we must consider the horse's own beauty, speed and strength. **(26)** .... truth, the picture we **(27)** .... most frequently moved by, in both art and literature, is actually a single image that combines all the advantages of the animal and its rider. An outstanding example of **(28)** .... is provided by the school of sculpture and painting in **(29)** .... the authority and personality of individuals is emphasised by the **(30)** .... that they are on horseback.

PART 3

For questions **31–40***, complete the second sentence so that it has a similar meaning to the first sentence, using the word given.* **Do not change the word given***. You must use between two and five words, including the word given. There is an example at the beginning (***0***).*
Write **only** *the missing words* **on the separate answer sheet***.*

Example:

0   I last saw him at my 21st birthday party.
     since

     I .... my 21st birthday party.

The gap can be filled by the words 'haven't seen him since' so you write:

0	*haven't seen him since*	0	0 1 2

---

31 Do you know who this coat belongs to?
     coat

     Do you know .... is?

32 Jo's training accident meant she couldn't take part in the race.
     prevented

     Jo's training accident .... part in the race.

33 Cyclists are not allowed to ride on the station platform.
     must

     Bicycles .... on the station platform.

34 To Alan's amazement, the passport office was closed when he arrived.
     find

     Alan .... the passport office closed when he arrived.

35 It isn't necessary to book tickets for the show in advance.
     need

     You .... tickets for the show in advance.

36 The top shelf was so high that the children couldn't reach it.
high

The top shelf was .... the children to reach.

37 I'd prefer you to start work next week.
rather

I .... work next week.

38 'Do you remember what you have to do?' the teacher asked her class.
what

The teacher asked her class if .... to do.

39 It's unusual for Carol to get angry with her staff.
hardly

Carol .... temper with her staff.

40 There is no ice-cream left.
run

We .... ice-cream.

PART 4

*For questions **41–55**, read the text below and look carefully at each line. Some of the lines are correct, and some have a word which should not be there. If a line is correct, put a tick (✓) by the number **on the separate answer sheet**. If a line has a word which should **not** be there, write the word **on the separate answer sheet**. There are two examples at the beginning (**0** and **00**).*

Examples:

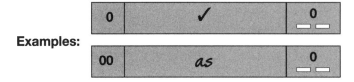

0	✓	0
00	*as*	0

A LETTER OF APOLOGY

Dear Richard,

0	Thanks very much for your letter. It was good to hear
00	all your news and I'm glad that your family are all as well.
41	It's very kind of you to invite for me to stay with you in
42	the June, but unfortunately my final exams are that month
43	and I don't yet know of the dates. I think they may be in
44	the week that you've suggested. In any case, judging
45	from my last Geography results, I will need to be studying
46	rather more than having a good time with my friends.
47	As soon as I will get the dates, I'll let you know but I
48	don't much expect I'll be able to come. Perhaps we'll be
49	able to get something organised for July. It's a long time
50	ever since we got together and I'd love to catch up on
51	what has been happening to you. If only your parents
52	don't want their house full of visitors in the holiday, you
53	could come over to stay with me. There's a plenty of
54	room and the house is just at a short bike ride from the
55	beach, so there would be lots to do. Let me know it if you
	think this is a good idea.
	Best wishes

PART 5

*For questions **56–65**, read the text below. Use the word given in capitals at the end of each line to form a word that fits in the space in the same line. There is an example at the beginning (**0**). Write your word **on the separate answer sheet**.*

Example:

0	*natural*	0

AN IMPORTANT ENGLISH TOWN

The site of the town of Winchester was a **(0)** .... place for a   **NATURE**
(56) .... , at the point where a river cut through the chalk of the   **SETTLE**
(57) .... hillsides. A simple camp at St Catherine's Hill was the   **SOUTH**
(58) .... known use of the site. This was followed by an Iron Age   **EARLY**
hill-fort, but this was left **(59)** .... by 100 BC. It was the Romans who   **INHABIT**
finally established the town and **(60)** .... it with a defensive wall for   **ROUND**
the protection of their people and trade.

With the **(61)** .... of its first cathedral in the seventh century, the   **BUILD**
town became an important **(62)** .... centre. Later, King Alfred, who   **RELIGION**
had **(63)** .... pushed back the invading Danes, moved his palace   **SUCCESS**
to Winchester. The town then experienced rapid **(64)** .... , and   **DEVELOP**
its **(65)** .... role in English history was underlined in 1066 when the   **CENTRE**
conquering Normans, like Alfred, made Winchester their capital.

PAPER 4   LISTENING (approximately 40 minutes)

PART 1

You will hear people talking in eight different situations.
For questions 1–8, choose the best answer, A, B or C.

1   You are walking round a market when you hear this woman talking to a customer.
    What is she doing?

    A   asking the customer's opinion

    B   offering a cheap sample

    C   explaining a price rise

	1

2   You're in the doctor's waiting room when you overhear the nurse on the phone.
    Why didn't she send off the notes?

    A   She didn't know they were wanted.

    B   It isn't part of her job to do it.

    C   She didn't know which notes to send.

	2

3   You're in a gallery when you hear these women talking.
    What are they looking at?

    A   a bowl

    B   a lamp

    C   a vase

	3

4   You are visiting a large company and you hear two people talking.
    What are they discussing?

    A   a personal computer

    B   a typewriter

    C   a CD player

	4

5 Listen to this clerk at a station booking office.
Which is the cheapest ticket?

A a period return

B an ordinary return

C a Rover

	5

6 These friends are talking about a film.
Who will go to see it?

A both of them

B neither of them

C the girl

	6

7 These people are talking about a colleague.
What's his problem?

A His boss is unfair to him.

B He has been ill.

C He has too much to do.

	7

8 Listen to this woman phoning a travel agent.
What does she want to do?

A cancel her booking

B postpone her holiday

C change her destination

	8

PART 2

You will hear an interview about sports facilities.
For questions 9–18, fill in the answers on the questionnaire.

Where does the interviewee live?	9
What is the interviewee's occupation?	10
How often does s/he use a public swimming pool?	11
What does s/he feel about the opening times?	12
What about entry charges?	13
What does s/he feel about existing facilities?	14
What would s/he most like to see added to these?	15
What other sports should be catered for locally?	16
Where should money for improvements come from?	17
Who should be able to use the pool free?	18

PART 3

You will hear five people talking to someone they have just met.
For questions 19–23, choose which of the people A–F each speaker is talking to.
Use the letters only once. There is one extra letter which you do not need to use.

A a tenant

B a neighbour

C a holidaymaker

D a colleague at work

E a trainee

F a hotel guest

Speaker 1		**19**
Speaker 2		**20**
Speaker 3		**21**
Speaker 4		**22**
Speaker 5		**23**

You will hear a discussion between Andy and Sharon about advertising their small business.

*For questions **24–30**, decide which of the statements are true and which are false and write **T** for True or **F** for False in the box provided.*

24   They have decided to spend some money on advertising.
| | 24 |

25   Their customers found their last advertisement boring.
| | 25 |

26   They need to attract better staff.
| | 26 |

27   Andy has contacted the local newspaper.
| | 27 |

28   They agree to advertise once a week.
| | 28 |

29   Sharon thinks a professional delivery company would cost too much.
| | 29 |

30   Andy agrees they should employ students.
| | 30 |

PAPER 5 SPEAKING (14 minutes)

Part 1

You tell the examiner about yourself. The examiner may ask you questions such as: Where are you from? How do you usually spend your free time? What are your plans for the future? Your partner does the same.

Part 2

The examiner gives you two pictures to look at and asks you to talk about them for about a minute. Your partner does the same with two different pictures.

Part 3

The examiner gives you a photograph or drawing to look at with your partner. You are asked to solve a problem or come to a decision about something in the picture. For example, you might be asked to decide the best way to use some rooms in a language school. You discuss the problem together.

Part 4

You are asked more questions connected with your discussion in Part 3. For example, you might be asked to talk about the best ways of studying.

Practice Test 3

PAPER 1   READING (1 hour 15 minutes)

PART 1

*You are going to read a newspaper article about women and technical subjects. Choose from the list (**A–I**) the sentence which best summarises each part (**1–7**) of the article. There is one extra sentence which you do not need to use. There is an example at the beginning (**0**).*
*Mark your answers **on the separate answer sheet**.*

<table>
<tr><td>**A**</td><td>Women often can't find, or don't think of looking for, the opportunities they need.</td></tr>
<tr><td>**B**</td><td>Women are needed in jobs that require a technological background.</td></tr>
<tr><td>**C**</td><td>Women study basic subjects alongside more specialised ones.</td></tr>
<tr><td>**D**</td><td>At the end of the course, women usually find jobs in local industry.</td></tr>
<tr><td>**E**</td><td>Women who want to change their jobs cannot because they have the wrong qualifications.</td></tr>
<tr><td>**F**</td><td>It is difficult to convince women and girls that they should take up scientific subjects.</td></tr>
<tr><td>**G**</td><td>In one training centre, the women are very eager to study scientific and technological subjects.</td></tr>
<tr><td>**H**</td><td>It is often difficult to obtain a place on a course.</td></tr>
<tr><td>**I**</td><td>My early interests were not developed.</td></tr>
</table>

Workface

A second chance to pick up a screwdriver, plug into the future and join the enthusiasts back at school

0	*I*

'I'VE always been interested in electronics and I often opened up the TV or the hi-fi to have a look. But I wasn't encouraged at school; I was the only girl in the Physics class and I felt lonely and depressed.'

1	

Susan Veerasamie's experience is typical of many. Eager to be the same as their friends, teenage girls shy away from technical and science subjects at school and then after a few years in a low-paid dead-end, 'woman's' job, they find they haven't got the qualifications to enable them to change course.

2	

The Haringey Women's Training and Education Centre, which Susan Veerasamie attends, is one of a handful of centres offering women a second chance to study technological and engineering subjects. It is housed in part of a former secondary school in north London and I doubt that the building has ever seen such keen students.

3	

The Centre provides courses in electronics, computing, the construction trades and science and technical skills, and everyone attends classes in numeracy, English and business practice.

4	

Hopefully, when they have completed their courses, the Centre's students will have gained enough confidence and basic skills to find a job or go on to further study. Nevertheless, getting on to a course at a college of further education is not easy if you don't have the required qualifications. The Manpower Services Commission offers courses in craft and technological skills which are open to everyone who is unemployed. However, places are often in high demand and the courses offered depend on the needs of local industry.

5	

There are other introductory and 'taster' courses similar to the Haringey Centre's around the country but they are scarce. It is often difficult for women to find a course that meets their needs and there is little to attract the attention of those who may never have considered work in the engineering and technological fields.

6	

The problem is how to persuade girls to broaden their options, and also to introduce training and retraining to women who have chosen more traditional paths, only to find the way to improved employment prospects closed or, at best, unsatisfying.

7	

Encouraging women to enter traditional 'male' work areas in greater numbers in this way is not only important for the women themselves, in that it offers a route into higher paid work, but it is also important for the country as a whole. There is a general skills shortage in the technological industries. We need these women's enthusiasm and ability.

*You are going to read an extract about children's fiction. For questions **8–15**, choose
the answer (**A, B, C** or **D**) which you think fits best according to the text.
Mark your answers **on the separate answer sheet**.*

What is good writing for children?

The children's publishers will tell you they look for 'good writing'. What exactly do they mean?

Before you send a story you have written to any publisher at all, your severest critic ought to be you yourself. To have a chance of succeeding in the competitive market of children's fiction, you should constantly be aware, every single time you sit down at your word-processor, of the need to produce 'good, original writing'. A difficult task, maybe, but one which hopefully we will help you to achieve.

To begin with, let us try to pin down exactly what publishers mean when they talk about 'good writing' for children. A useful starting point would be to take a look at some of the children's books which won literary prizes last year. Reading these books is one of the easiest and most enjoyable ways of: (a) finding out what individual publishers are publishing at the moment, and (b) learning a few tricks of the trade from well-established professionals. It goes without saying, of course, that slavishly copying the style and subject matter of a successful author is usually a recipe for disaster. Nor should you become downhearted after reading a particularly brilliant piece of work, and miserably think you will never be able to match up to those standards. Remember, overnight success is rare – most successful children's authors will have struggled long and hard to learn their trade. Read these books as a critic; note down the things you enjoyed or admired, as well as areas where you feel there was possibly room for improvement. After all, nobody is perfect, not even a successful, prize-winning author.

Possibly the toughest challenge is right at the youngest end of the age range – the picture book. The would-be author/illustrator is attempting to create an exciting story out of the narrow, limited, everyday world of a young child's experience – not easy at all. The whole storyline has to be strong enough to keep the reader turning the pages, yet simple enough to fit into a few pages. Another problem for the new picture-book author is that it can seem that every subject and every approach has been done to death, with nothing new left to say. Add to this the fact that printing costs are high because of full colour illustrations, which means that the publisher will probably want a text that suits the international market to increase sales, and a novel for ten-year olds, with hardly any pictures at all, starts to look much more inviting.

You would be forgiven for wondering if there are any truly original plots left to impress publishers with. But remember that, in many ways, it is the writer's own personal style, and intelligent handling of a subject that can change a familiar, overworked plot into something original and fresh. To illustrate this, read *The Enchanted Horse* by Magdalen Nabb. A young girl called Irina finds an old wooden horse in a junk shop, takes it home and treats it as if it was real. Soon it magically starts to come to life … Sounds familiar? The magic object that comes alive is a story-line that has been used in hundreds of other children's stories. So why does it succeed here? The answer is that Magdalen Nabb has created a strong, believable character in the lonely, unhappy heroine Irina, and the descriptions of her relationship with the wooden horse are poetic and touching.

So, to return to the question asked at the beginning: What exactly is 'good writing' for children? The answer is that it is writing which is fresh, exciting and unpredictable, and which gives a new and original angle on what might be a well-worn subject. But do not be put off if you feel that you simply cannot match up to all these requirements. While there is obviously no substitute for talent, and the ability to come up with suitable ideas, many of the techniques for improving and polishing your manuscript can be learned.

8 Why does the article advise people to look at prize-winning books?
  A to copy the author's style
  B to realise what a high standard needs to be reached
  C to get an idea of what might be successful
  D to find out how to trick publishers

9 What do most successful children's authors have in common?
  A They did not get depressed by early failures.
  B They have learned how to be critical of other authors' work.
  C They find it easy to think of storylines that will sell.
  D They have worked hard to become well-known.

10 Why is the picture book the most difficult to write?
  A There is a limited range of subjects available.
  B Young children cannot follow storylines easily.
  C The pictures need to be exciting.
  D Children want to be able to read it quickly.

11 What looks 'more inviting' in line 54?
  A the international market
  B the increased sales
  C the novel for ten-year-olds
  D the type of pictures

12 The book about Irina is successful
  A because of the unusual way magic is used.
  B because of the way the character is described.
  C because the story has not been told before.
  D because the pictures bring the story to life.

13 What does 'it' refer to in line 68?
  A the storyline
  B the magic object
  C the horse
  D the children's story

14 What conclusion does the writer of the text come to?
  A Anyone can learn to write a good story.
  B The subject matter is the most important consideration.
  C If you have natural ability, you can learn the rest.
  D Some published fiction is badly written.

15 Why was this text written?
  A to explain what kind of books children like to read
  B to give advice to people who want to write children's fiction
  C to discourage new authors from being too optimistic
  D to persuade new authors to get away from old ideas

PART 3

*You are going to read a magazine article about bodyclocks. Seven sentences have been removed from the article. Choose from the sentences (**A–H**) the one which fits each gap (**16–21**). There is one extra sentence which you do not need to use. There is an example at the beginning (**0**).*
*Mark your answers **on the separate answer sheet**.*

RHYTHM OF LIFE

Scientists have discovered that our bodies operate on a 25-hour day. So tuning into your bodyclock can make things really tick, says Jenny Hope, *Daily Mail* Medical Correspondent.

Choosing the right time to sleep, the correct moment to make decisions, the best hour to eat – and even go into hospital – could be your key to perfect health.

Centuries after man discovered the rhythms of the planets and the cycles of crops, scientists have learned that we too live by precise rhythms that govern the ebb and flow of everything from our basic bodily functions to mental skills. **0** | *H* |

But it's not just the experts who are switching on to the way our bodies work. **16** | | Prince Charles consults a chart which tells him when he will be at his peak on a physical, emotional and intellectual level. Boxer Frank Bruno is another who charts his bio-rhythms to plan for big fights.

17 | | Sleep, blood pressure, hormone levels and heartbeat all follow their own clocks, which may bear only slight relation to our man-made 24-hour cycle.

Research shows that in laboratory experiments when social signals and, most crucially, light indicators such as dawn are taken away, people lose touch with the 24-hour clock and sleeping patterns change. **18** | |

In the real world, light and dark keep adjusting internal clocks to the 24-hour day. **19** | | As it falls from a 10 p.m. high of 37.2°C to a pre-dawn low of 36.1°C, mental functions fall too. This is a key reason why shift work can cause so many problems – both for workers and their organisations.

20 | | The three operators in the control room worked alternating weeks of day, evening and night shifts – a dangerous combination which never gave their bodies' natural rhythms a chance to settle down. Investigators believe this caused the workers to over-look a warning light and fail to close an open valve.

Finding the secret of what makes us tick has long fascinated scientists and work done over the last decade has yielded important clues.

| 21 | | For example, the time we eat may be important if we want to maximise intellectual or sporting performance. There is already evidence suggesting that the time when medicine is given to patients affects how well it works.

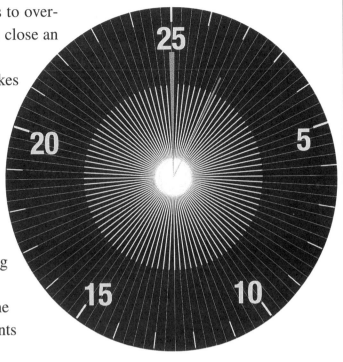

A   Temperature and heartbeat cycles lengthen and settle into 'days' lasting about 25 hours.

B   The most famous example is the nuclear accident at Three Mile Island in the US.

C   But the best indicator of performance is body temperature.

D   Leading experts say every aspect of human biology is influenced by daily rhythms.

E   Dr Michael Stroud is one of the few people alive who can genuinely claim to have tested their bodyclocks to the limit.

F   The aim is to help us become more efficient.

G   An increasing number of people study the state of their bio-rhythms before making their daily plans.

H   Man is a prisoner of time.

PART 4

*You are going to read about four competitions which offer holidays as prizes. For questions **22–35**, choose from the competitions (**A–D**). Some of the competitions may be chosen more than once. When more than one answer is required, these may be given in any order. There is an example at the beginning (**0**).*
*Mark your answers **on the separate answer sheet**.*

Which holiday prize offers you the chance to:

visit a desert?	**0**	*B*
go to the seaside?	**22**	**23**
stay in a new hotel?	**24**	
have a chance to exercise?	**25**	**26**
be sure of seeing some animals?	**27**	
look around the city and see something of the countryside?	**28**	
stay longer than a week?	**29**	**30**

Which competition extract:

describes what will happen on the flight?	**31**
says there is more than one prize?	**32**
offers to take the winner on a historical tour as part of the prize?	**33**
offers a holiday which includes all food?	**34**
is advertising a particular product?	**35**

A

clearly CANADA

Vancouver is a stylish, metropolitan centre with the scenic Pacific Ocean at its feet and impressive coastal mountains behind. To give you the chance to experience its delights for yourself, *Options* magazine has teamed up with 'Clearly Canadian' – a blend of native Canadian fruit flavours and sparkling water – to bring you this great competition.

The lucky prizewinner and guest will enjoy a fabulous ten-day getaway, flying direct to Vancouver with Canadian Airlines. On board, they will enjoy an in-flight movie while sampling a delicious meal served on real china.

Accommodation for the winner and guest will be at Shangri-La's Pacific Palisades Hotel, one of Vancouver's first-class hotels. They will enjoy a luxury executive suite, with stunning views over the harbour, and use of the hotel's health club and pool. Ten runners-up will receive a bottle of 'Clearly Canadian' and an exclusively designed T-shirt.

While in Vancouver, you will have many opportunities to sample Canadian city life. Browse in fashionable shops, linger in sidewalk cafés or relax on the beach.

Buy this magazine next week and we'll give you the competition details.

B

GO WILD!

NAMIBIA is a country of desert dunes, wide horizons and clear skies. Enter this competition and you and a friend could be on your way.

Your one-week prize holiday begins at Heathrow airport where you will board an Air Namibia plane bound for the capital. Air Namibia Holidays' magnificent Namibia tour will take you straight to the very heart of the country. All travel arrangements will be taken care of – all you have to do is sit back and enjoy the scenery. You'll start with a drive to the Namib Desert Park, then go on to see the pelicans, flamingos and terns at Walvis Bay lagoon, before heading for the coastal resort of Swakopmund.

The highlight of the tour is a safari through Etosha National Park, home to thousands of elephants, zebras, giraffes and antelopes as well as lions, leopards, cheetahs and rhinos.

All meals are included throughout the holiday and you'll stay in some of Namibia's best lodges and camps.

We just ask you to think of

C

WIN A FABULOUS HOLIDAY FOR TWO!

Visit the deserted city of Fatehpur Sikri. Stand back in amazement as you marvel at the wildlife reserves where you'll see exotic birds and possibly even a tiger! These are just some of the sights you'll experience on the thrilling ten-day 'Moghul Highlights' holiday.

The holiday begins with a tour of Old Delhi. Proceeding by road to Agra, you'll stop on the way to see the Tomb of Akbar. Moving on to see Agra Fort and the beautiful Taj Mahal on the banks of the Yamuna River, your group will then explore Akbar's red sandstone city, Fatehpur Sikri, built in 1574. Lunch will be taken in the Keoladeo National Park at Bharatpur, a birdwatcher's paradise.

This fantastic holiday package includes the return flight from Heathrow to Delhi, the holiday tour and insurance. All breakfasts while in India are included but holiday participants will need to buy meals at local restaurants in India.

To find out what you have to do

D

win *a week of luxury in* **BUDAPEST**

The lucky winner and a friend will fly direct to Budapest International Airport and will then be taken to The Palace Hotel, a luxurious hotel set in its own large park on the banks of the river Danube. The Palace Hotel is just two years old – a modern addition to the ancient skyline.

You'll enjoy five nights' bed and breakfast accommodation in a room that overlooks the river Danube, and will be treated to dinner in the Café Suisse. We have not ordered lunch for you but it is also available in the restaurant.

The week in Budapest can be spent at leisure either relaxing in the hotel and its grounds, or wandering around the superb shopping arcade. Alternatively, The Palace Hotel has extensive health club facilities – including an indoor pool and a free steam bath. If you're feeling really energetic, you could play a game of tennis or jog around the grounds on the two-mile landscaped track.

To make sure you take in some of the sights of Budapest, you may wish to book at very reasonable cost a day's sightseeing with President Holidays.

Look at the next page to see what you have to do.

PAPER 2 WRITING (1 hour 30 minutes)

PART 1

*You **must** answer this question.*

1   You are on holiday at the Bayview Hotel and have decided to come back to the same place next year. You have kept a diary during your stay. Part of this is shown below with the holiday advertisement which you cut out. You have made some notes on the advertisement.

Read the diary and the advertisement. Then write a letter to your friend, persuading him or her to come with you next year. Use the information given to say what you could do together.

MONDAY

Sailing – first time for me!

Evening – new Spielberg film

TUESDAY

Coach trip to old town

Evening – disco

Bayview Hotel
Family-run hotel on sea front. Restaurant, bars.

friendly people   *good food*

Write a **letter** of between **120–180** words in an appropriate style on the next page. Do not write any addresses.

PART 1

PART 2

Write an answer to **one** *of the questions* **2–5** *in this part. Write your answer in* **120–180** *words in an appropriate style on the next page, putting the question number in the box.*

2 As part of a new series, an educational magazine has invited readers to write articles calle͏   ͏d why I started learning English. Write an **article** based on y͏   ͏rience.

3 Your teacher has ͏   ͏rite a story which includes the sentence **That was the moment w͏   ͏ was in the wrong place**. Write your **story**.

4 A local newspaper has invited   ͏urants from its readers. Write a **report** on a visit to **one** local res͏   ͏ort should cover the food, service, decoration and atmosphe͏   ͏nt, and should also comment on any problems you expe͏

5 Background reading texts

Answer **one** of the following two questions bas͏   ͏   ͏ of **one** of the set books (see p. v). Write the title of the book͏   ͏t͏   ͏ number box.

Either **(a)** Describe some of the most important actio͏   ͏e b͏ explain how they help to develop the story.

or   **(b)** Would the book make a good film? Say why or ͏   ͏t.

PART 2

Question	

....
....
....
....
....
....
....
....
....
....
....
....
....
....
....
....
....
....
....
....
....
....
....
....
....
....

PAPER 3   USE OF ENGLISH (1 hour 15 minutes)

PART 1

*For questions **1–15**, read the text below and decide which answer **A, B, C** or **D**
best fits each space. There is an example at the beginning (**0**).
Mark your answers **on the separate answer sheet**.*

Example:

0   A sigh   **B** yawn   **C** cough   **D** sneeze

0	A	B	C	D
	▬	▭	▭	▭

HELEN AND MARTIN

With a thoughtful **(0)** .... , Helen turned away from the window and walked back to
her favourite armchair. **(1)** .... her brother never arrive? For a brief moment, she
wondered if she really cared that much.

Over the years Helen had given **(2)** .... waiting for Martin to take an interest in her.
Her feelings for him had gradually **(3)** .... until now, as she sat waiting for him, she
experienced no more than a sister's **(4)** .... to see what had **(5)** .... of her brother.

Almost without **(6)** .... , Martin had lost his job with a busy publishing company after
spending the last eight years in New York as a key figure in the US office. Somehow
the two of them hadn't **(7)** .... to keep in touch and, left alone, Helen had slowly
found her **(8)** .... in her own judgement growing. **(9)** .... the wishes of her parents, she
had left university halfway **(10)** .... her course and now, to the astonishment of the
whole family, she was **(11)** .... a fast-growing reputation in the pages of respected art
magazines and was actually earning enough to live **(12)** .... from her paintings.

Of course, she **(13)** .... no pleasure in Martin's sudden misfortune, but she couldn't
(14) .... looking forward to her brother's arrival with **(15)** .... satisfaction at what she
had achieved.

1 **A** Could   **B** Should   **C** Would   **D** Ought

2 **A** in   **B** up   **C** out   **D** away

3 **A** depressed   **B** weakened   **C** lowered   **D** fainted

4 **A** wonder   **B** idea   **C** curiosity   **D** regard

5 **A** become   **B** developed   **C** arisen   **D** changed

6 **A** caution   **B** warning   **C** advice   **D** signal

7 **A** minded   **B** concerned   **C** worried   **D** bothered

8 **A** dependence   **B** confidence **C** certainty   **D** courage

9 **A** Ignoring   **B** Omitting   **C** Avoiding   **D** Preventing

10 **A** along   **B** down   **C** through   **D** across

11 **A** gaining   **B** reaching   **C** starting   **D** opening

12 **A** for   **B** by   **C** with   **D** on

13 **A** made   **B** took   **C** drew   **D** formed

14 **A** help   **B** miss   **C** fail   **D** drop

15 **A** soft   **B** fine   **C** quiet   **D** still

PART 2

*For questions **16–30**, read the text below and think of the word which best fits each space. Use only **one** word in each space. There is an example at the beginning (**0**).*
*Write your word **on the separate answer sheet**.*

Example:

0	*most*	0

CYCLING ROUND CORNERS

Taking a corner is one of the **(0)** .... satisfying moves you can make on a bike. It's fun, it's exciting, and it also happens **(16)** .... be one of the hardest things to learn. Even **(17)** .... experienced rider can always **(18)** .... improvements in this area. Good cornering is the ability to cycle through a turn **(19)** .... full control, no matter **(20)** .... the conditions. This might mean racing **(21)** .... high speed down a winding descent, but just **(22)** .... important is the ability to deal with a slow, sharp turn **(23)** .... you are touring with lots of luggage. In **(24)** .... these cases there are some general points to remember.

When going very slowly you can steer through a corner using your hands on the handlebars **(25)** .... , as speed increases, any sudden turning of the front wheel **(26)** .... likely to result in loss of control. To avoid **(27)** .... effect, a bike must be turned by leaning it, by steering with the body instead of the hands. On sharp turns of more **(28)** .... about 70 degrees, even this is **(29)** .... enough: you must also lower your body towards the bike as much as you **(30)** .... to help keep it from slipping out from under you. When you are cornering correctly you will feel very solid. It's a good feeling – exciting but not really dangerous.

PART 3

For questions **31–40**, *complete the second sentence so that it has a similar meaning to the first sentence, using the word given.* **Do not change the word given**. *You must use between two and five words, including the word given. There is an example at the beginning (***0***).*
Write **only** *the missing words* **on the separate answer sheet**.

Example:

0   I last saw him at my 21st birthday party.
      since

      I .... my 21st birthday party.

The gap can be filled by the words 'haven't seen him since' so you write:

0	*haven't seen him since*	0	0 1 2

---

31   There's no point in asking George to help.
       worth

       It .... George to help.

32   Harry couldn't get his parents' permission to buy a motorbike.
       let

       Harry's parents .... a motorbike.

33   'Where have I left my sunglasses, David?' asked Susan.
       where

       Susan asked David .... sunglasses.

34   John's behaviour at the party annoyed me.
       John

       I was annoyed by the .... at the party.

35   It's a good thing you lent me the money or I would have had to go to the bank.
       you

       I would have had to go to the bank .... me the money.

36 Matthew didn't listen to what his doctor told him.
notice

Matthew took .... advice.

37 Sheila had to finish the accounts and write several letters as well.
addition

Sheila had to finish the accounts .... several letters.

38 When he was a child in Australia, Mark went swimming almost every day.
his

Mark went swimming almost every day .... in Australia.

39 Let's visit the museum this afternoon.
go

Why .... the museum this afternoon?

40 Valerie found it hard to concentrate on her book because of the noise.
difficulty

Valerie .... her book because of the noise.

PART 4

*For questions **41–55**, read the text below and look carefully at each line. Some of the lines are correct, and some have a word which should not be there. If a line is correct, put a tick (✓) by the number **on the separate answer sheet**. If a line has a word which should **not** be there, write the word **on the separate answer sheet**. There are two examples at the beginning (**0** and **00**).*

Examples:

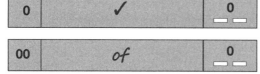

A PLACE WORTH VISITING

0	The Welsh National Folk Museum in Cardiff is one of the
00	most interesting of places I've ever visited and it's situated in
41	a very pretty countryside. The museum has collected various
42	buildings from all over the country and brought them together
43	in the grounds of a historic manor house, near where they have
44	been carefully rebuilt one brick by brick to look just like they
45	did in their original position. Then the interiors they have
46	been furnished in period style, and many interesting old tools
47	and other everyday household objects are on the display
48	in this realistic setting. It's fascinating to walk away from
49	building to building, imagining about the way people used to
50	live since years ago. Large families often lived in the tiniest
51	of cottages, sometimes even sharing in the space with the
52	domestic animals which were of such an importance to them.
53	You can go around the manor house as well, but in my opinion
54	there is no little to distinguish this from many other historic
55	houses elsewhere. It does have a much comfortable tea-room,
	however, which is very welcome after all that walking.

PART 5

*For questions **56–65**, read the text below. Use the word given in capitals at the end of each line to form a word that fits in the space in the same line. There is an example at the beginning (**0**). Write your word **on the separate answer sheet**.*

Example: | 0 | *construction* | 0 |

THE FUTURE OF TALL BUILDINGS

Architects responsible for the **(0)** .... of many skyscrapers believe	**CONSTRUCT**
that a tall building must always have a certain minimum **(56)** .... but	**WIDE**
that there is no limit to its absolute **(57)** .... . This means that the	**HIGH**
skyscrapers of the future are likely to be even taller.	
Engineers agree with this, but there is **(58)** .... over the best shape for	**AGREE**
very tall, slim buildings. The effects of wind **(59)** .... mean that	**PRESS**
cylindrical designs have enjoyed some **(60)** .... in recent years, and	**POPULAR**
these are quite pleasing to the eye. **(61)** .... , however, the ideal	**FORTUNATE**
shape is an ugly square with heavily rounded corners.	
Would these tall buildings of the future offer more than a **(62)**	**WONDER**
view? Some believe tall towers could contain all the **(63)** .... for	**REQUIRE**
modern living. The **(64)** .... of these vertical villages would travel up	**INHABIT**
and down between their home and work zones and would **(65)**	**RARE**
need to journey to ground level.	

PAPER 4   LISTENING (approximately 40 minutes)

PART 1

You will hear people talking in eight different situations.
For questions **1–8**, *choose the best answer* **A, B** *or* **C.**

1   You are visiting a trade exhibition when you hear a speaker at one of the stands.
What is he demonstrating?

   A   a watch

   B   a lock

   C   a burglar alarm

	1

2   This girl is talking about a party.
What was it like?

   A   boring

   B   too crowded

   C   noisy

	2

3   Listen to this hotel receptionist talking on the phone.
Who is she talking to?

   A   a friend

   B   a guest

   C   her employer

	3

4   You hear this advertisement on the radio.
Who is it aimed at?

   A   people who have plenty of money

   B   people who might borrow money

   C   people who need to save money

	4

5 Listen to these students talking about their holiday work.
Where are they working?

A a library

B an office

C a shop

5

6 Listen to this man.
Where has he been?

A to the gym

B to the dentist

C to the barber

6

7 You hear this woman talking on the radio.
What is she discussing?

A music

B a picture

C architecture

7

8 You hear this man talking to a shop assistant.
Why is he annoyed?

A His pen has leaked in his pocket.

B HIs pen has been repaired recently.

C His pen was very expensive.

8

PART 2

You will hear a teacher telling new students about their course.
For questions 9–18, listen to what she says and complete the notes.

Classes in Studio every afternoon

Room 51 on   [9]

On Fridays can use   [10]   for private study

Extra courses: Monday   [11]

Tuesday   [12]

Wednesday   [13]

Application forms from   [14]

Saturday course on computer-aided design

Open to   [15]   students only

Must provide own   [16]

Short absences, phone   [17]

More than two days, write to   [18]

PART 3

You will hear five people saying thank you.
*For questions **19–23**, choose which of **A–F** each speaker is talking about. Use the letters only once. There is one extra letter which you do not need to use.*

A good teaching

B support in a difficult task

Speaker 1		19

C a warning

Speaker 2		20

Speaker 3		21

D a present

Speaker 4		22

E a piece of information

Speaker 5		23

F a loan

PART 4

You will hear a radio discussion about a wildlife park.
For questions 24–30, decide which of the choices A, B or C is the correct answer.

24 Where is South Glen?

   A   inside Glenside Park
   B   between the park and the main road
   C   near the park

[ ] 24

25 What does Ian say about Helen's plans?

   A   He doesn't like them.
   B   He doesn't understand them.
   C   He doesn't know what they are.

[ ] 25

26 Helen claims that, at present, visitors

   A   walk about in large groups.
   B   go all over the park.
   C   damage the plants.

[ ] 26

27 Why is it a problem for the staff to raise young birds?

   A   They lack the necessary skills.
   B   It costs a lot of money.
   C   There isn't the right equipment.

[ ] 27

28 Ian thinks it is ridiculous to

   A   encourage more visitors.
   B   make visitors pay an entrance fee.
   C   build fences round the animals.

[ ] 28

29 Helen says that fires

   A   have been started by accident.
   B   are impossible to control.
   C   are a possible danger.

[ ] 29

30 Ian believes that the villagers nowadays

   A   are more aware of the environment than
       their grandparents.
   B   show enough respect for the environment.
   C   have become careless about the environment.

[ ] 30

PAPER 5   SPEAKING (14 minutes)

Part 1

You tell the examiner about yourself. The examiner may ask you questions such as: Where are you from? How do you usually spend your free time? What are your plans for the future? Your partner does the same.

Part 2

The examiner gives you two pictures to look at and asks you to talk about them for about a minute. Your partner does the same with two different pictures.

Part 3

The examiner gives you a photograph or drawing to look at with your partner. You are asked to solve a problem or come to a decision about something in the picture. For example, you might be asked to decide the best way to use some rooms in a language school. You discuss the problem together.

Part 4

You are asked more questions connected with your discussion in Part 3. For example, you might be asked to talk about the best ways of studying.

Practice Test 4

PAPER 1   READING (1 hour 15 minutes)

PART 1

*You are going to read a magazine article about pollution of the atmosphere. Choose the most suitable heading from the list (**A–I**) for each part (**1–7**) of the article. There is one extra heading which you do not need to use. There is an example at the beginning (**0**).*
*Mark your answers **on the separate answer sheet**.*

A	Before ozone existed
B	Repair gets slower
C	People ignore warnings
D	Ozone hole a certainty
E	The future is our responsibility
F	The function of the ozone layer
G	Delayed reactions
H	Humans to blame
I	Strange results

The ozone layer
What is it? What is happening to it?

0	*I*

In September 1982, Dr Joe Farman, a British scientist working in the Antarctic, found that a dramatic change had taken place in the atmosphere above his research station on the ice continent. His instruments, set up to measure the amounts of a chemical called ozone in the atmosphere, seemed to go wild. Over just a few days they recorded that half the ozone had disappeared.

1

He couldn't believe his eyes, so he came back to Britain to get a new instrument to check his findings. But when he returned the following year at the same time, the same thing happened. He had discovered a hole in the ozone layer – an invisible shield in the upper atmosphere – that turned out to extend over an area of the sky as wide as the United States and as deep as Mount Everest is high. When he published his findings in scientific journals, they caused a sensation. Scientists blamed pollution for causing the ozone hole.

2

The ozone layer is between 15 and 40 kilometres up in the atmosphere, higher than most aeroplanes fly. This region contains most of the atmosphere's ozone, which is a special form of the gas oxygen. Ozone has the unique ability to stop certain dangerous invisible rays from the sun from reaching the Earth's surface – rather like a pair of sunglasses filters out bright sunlight. These rays are known as ultra-violet radiation. This damages living cells, causing sunburn and more serious diseases. The ozone layer is vital to life on the surface of the Earth.

3

Until the ozone layer formed, about two thousand million years ago, it was impossible for any living thing to survive on the surface of the planet. All life was deep in the oceans. But once oxygen was formed in the air, and some of that oxygen turned to ozone, plants and animals could begin to move on to land.

4

But now humans are damaging the ozone layer for the first time. In the past ten years, scientists have discovered that some man-made gases, used in everything from refrigerators and aerosols to fire extinguishers, are floating up into the ozone layer and destroying the ozone. The most common of these gases are called chlorofluorocarbons (CFCs).

5

The damage is worst over Antarctica, and near the North Pole, where scientists have seen small holes appear for a short time each spring since 1989. So far, these holes have healed up again within a few weeks by natural processes in the atmosphere that create more ozone. But each year, it seems to take longer for the healing to be completed. Also, all round the planet, there now seems to be less ozone in the ozone layer than even a few years ago.

6

The first new international law to stop people making or using CFCs was the Montreal Protocol, agreed by most of the world's governments in 1987. Since then, there have been new controls on other chemicals that destroy ozone. The problem is that it takes roughly eight years for CFCs, which are released when an old fridge is broken up, to reach the ozone layer. That is why, despite all the cuts, ozone holes were deeper than ever around both the North and South Poles in 1993. Amounts of CFCs in the atmosphere will continue to rise for another five years, say scientists.

7

Every year, the atmosphere will attempt to repair damage to the ozone layer caused by our pollution. But we are stretching its capacity to recover to the limit. If we stop using all ozone-destroying chemicals within the next five years, it is likely to be at least the middle of the 21st century before the ozone hole stops forming over Antarctica each year. And, if we are to survive, we all have to face the problem now.

PART 2

You are going to read an article about a woman called Rebecca Ridgway. For questions **8–14**, choose the answer (**A, B, C** or **D**) which you think fits best according to the text.

Mark your answers **on the separate answer sheet**.

Tea at Ardmore

To reach Ardmore and take tea with Rebecca Ridgway you must make an expedition; not, perhaps an expedition in the Ridgway class, involving months of painstaking planning, physical training, mental preparation; not, when it's underway, the same degree of discomfort or edge of danger, but a prolonged exercise in transport arrangements in order to reach her crofthouse on a roadless peninsula near Cape Wrath, in the north-west corner of Scotland.

Rebecca does have neighbours; most importantly her parents, John and Marie-Christine Ridgway and one or two other self-sufficient solitaries who have settled in the remains of the crofting community of Ardmore. The Ridgways' extended crofthouse is not only the nerve-centre of the John Ridgway Adventure School, but the living heart of a community whose isolation is intensified by every storm from the Atlantic.

I walk along the peninsula towards the white house above the lake. Although Rebecca now lives in the cottage next door, she is waiting with Marie-Christine in the family kitchen, mugs on the table and kettle on the boil. Mother and daughter share the same slight figures and delicate good looks, but their grace disguises a toughness built up on daily five-mile runs and early morning swims in the freezing waters of the lake.

'Dad's out there somewhere,' says Rebecca, waving a hand at the mountain view, 'with some of his students.' Each year, many of the same people turn up for the Adventure School's women's course of hillwalking and sailing. Ardmore welcomes are always warm, and there is news to exchange; much has happened to the Ridgways since we last met – not least Rebecca's voyage in a canoe round tempestuous Cape Horn. And now, after twenty-five seasons, the family are to close the school for a time and sail away (not exactly round the world, which John and Marie-Christine have already done when they raced their boat *English Rose VII*, or merely across the Atlantic, which John rowed with Chay Blyth in 1966), but round the land mass of South America. All three will make the eighteen-month voyage.

'Dad's been trying to persuade us to do this trip for years, although Mum always swore she'd never sail with him again. He makes everything so stressful and we all get dreadfully seasick. But we need a break from the school.'

The timing, from Rebecca's point of view, couldn't be more perfect. Since she canoed round the Horn and wrote the book which describes that singular adventure she feels 'the pressure is off'. For years she has been set the example of high-achieving parents – the driven, demanding ex-soldier and his deceptively fragile-looking wife, 'who is tougher than any of us, who works harder than any of us, who is my main inspiration' – and now feels she has done the 'something amazing' that was expected of her. 'Cape Horn was Mum's suggestion, although it's Dad who usually sets the toughest challenges.' Marie-Christine says her bright idea subsequently gave her more than a few sleepless nights.

'I suppose I've always been trying to prove something to Dad,' continues Rebecca, 'Not so much seek his approval as get some recognition. When I was younger I was a bit scared of this figure who marched about barking orders. But since we've travelled together – even sharing tents, for heaven's sake – I feel I've

got to know him better.'
 She is more relaxed about the future than she's ever been, less anxious about
90 'finding some kind of sensible qualification, like physiotherapy' to back up all the skills acquired on land and water, as shepherd, sailor, outdoor pursuits instructor and now writer fighting with a lap-top computer in the South Atlantic to send articles to the
95 *Daily Telegraph.*

8 It is a challenge to take tea with Rebecca Ridgway because
  A she lives in a dangerous spot.
  B it is difficult to persuade her to meet people.
  C she expects her guests to be very fit.
  D it is difficult to get to her home.

9 What does 'it' in line 6 refer to?
  A planning
  B tea
  C an exercise
  D an expedition

10 What are we told about Rebecca's home?
  A It is part of a settlement which used to be bigger.
  B It is the only house in the area.
  C It is shared with her parents.
  D It has been damaged in a storm.

11 What has Rebecca gained from the expedition round Cape Horn?
  A She has satisfied her parents' ambitions for her.
  B She has done something which her father was unable to achieve.
  C She has shown that she is stronger than her parents.
  D She has found out that she is a good writer.

12 What is her relationship with her father like?
  A She wishes he were less strict.
  B She wants him to notice her.
  C She is still frightened of him.
  D She wishes he were more like her mother.

13 What do we learn about Marie-Christine?
  A She is not as fit as she used to be.
  B She has never been very keen on sailing.
  C She is stronger than she looks.
  D She has always expected too much of her daughter.

14 How does Rebecca feel about the future?
  A She would like to have a change.
  B She is happy with the way things are going.
  C She wants to qualify as a physiotherapist.
  D She would like to have more time to write.

You are going to read a report of an interview with a film star. Eight sentences have been removed from the interview. Choose from the sentences (A–I) the one which fits each gap (15–21). There is one extra sentence which you do not need to use. There is an example at the beginning (0).
Mark your answers on the separate answer sheet.

Having a wonderful time

Judy Sloane meets Hollywood star **Douglas Fairbanks Junior**, son of the famous actor in silent movies. Fairbanks Junior has made an extremely successful career of his own.

Being brought up in a show business family, did you want to be an actor?

Well, it wasn't a show business family. [0][*I*] I couldn't help but be aware of it to a certain extent, because people would come around but the talk was very seldom shop-talk.

During your long and successful career you've certainly made the name Fairbanks your own, but when you were starting out was it a nuisance to you to be named after your father?

I think it probably was. It was a mixture in a way. It was useful in having the door open to get interviews, and to be allowed in to talk to the boss. [15][   ]

Were you and your father close?

Not at first. We were just shy of each other. I think we were always fond of each other. [16][   ] It wasn't until I was in my late twenties that we got to know each other very well.

Was your father a big influence in your life?

Not really, except I certainly took notice of his wonderful good nature with people. [17][   ] It was a natural friendliness, and I admired that and I probably wanted to give that same impression when I was young.

Out of all your father's films, do you have a favourite one?

I think my very favourite one is 'Thief Of Baghdad'. It was one of the finest films ever made by anybody. [18][   ] He was the guide and more or less the creator.

When did you know that you wanted to become an actor yourself?

When my mother and I were living abroad because it was cheaper, and mother's family had run out of money and we didn't know quite what to do, and somebody offered me a job! **19 [   ]** It was a job at Paramount Pictures to play in a film called 'Stephen Steps Out' for which I got $1,000 a week for two weeks.

Your role as Rupert of Hentzau in 'The Prisoner Of Zenda' was one of your greatest.

It was a wonderful, wonderful part. **20 [   ]** Then I had this offer to come back and do 'Prisoner Of Zenda'. I thought I'd better stick with this new company I'd started. My father was around and he said, 'Don't be a fool, you've got to go back, give up everything and play in "The Prisoner Of Zenda". It's the best part ever written'. And that decided me so I said, 'Yes, I will!'

Do you like the films they're making today?

The films themselves are all right. **21 [   ]** There are still some very fine films that are being made, but some of them are of questionable taste and I blame the public. Being a business and an industry, producers produce what people buy. If the public don't like it, they won't go, and the films will stop being produced.

A The same talents are there, it's the public that has changed.

B He was always very nice to everybody he talked to, and he didn't have to pretend.

C That's when I decided!

D It should have been better.

E But it didn't make the jobs any easier, in fact it probably made them harder, because they expected more than I was able to deliver at a young age.

F We didn't quite know how to show it.

G I think it's a great work of art, and although a lot of people are credited with having a hand in it, everybody did more or less as my father wanted.

H In fact I didn't know whether to accept it or not, because I'd been struggling for years to have my own company in Europe and I was just getting started on that.

I Only my father was in the business, and it wasn't brought home.

PART 4

You are going to read an article about a family trying a vegetarian diet. For questions 22–35, choose from the people in the box (A–E). Some of the people may be chosen more than once. When more than one answer is required, these may be given in any order.
There is an example at the beginning (0).
Mark your answers on the separate answer sheet.

A Sue	**B** Michael	**C** Jo	**D** Mary	**E** Robin

Which person:

changed one of the recipes?	0	*A*		
doesn't miss meat at all?	22		23	
prefers dishes which are not too spicy?	24			
was keenest to try the diet?	25			
likes dishes to have plenty of taste?	26			
finds the new diet allows less time for doing other things?	27			
misses some of the foods the family no longer eats?	28		29	
has found the experience very rewarding in terms of ideas?	30			
can't eat too much vegetarian food?	31			

already knew quite a lot about healthy eating? **32** ☐

likes to eat meat sometimes? **33** ☐ **34** ☐

will probably give up eating fish soon? **35** ☐

TAKING THE
plunge

If you're thinking about the idea of turning vegetarian but are afraid it may be boring or too expensive, think again. Last October, we challenged a typical meat-eating family to go on a vegetarian diet for at least seven days.

GET SET

Sue Kent, 42, said 'I'm quite health conscious when it comes to food, so we'd already started to cut out red meat.' To start the week, and put everyone in the right frame of mind, Sue prepared a family favourite, vegetarian chilli. The rest of the week followed like a dream. 'The recipes all went down extremely well,' says Sue. 'The tomato and pasta soup was popular, as was the pasta with tomato and mozzarella sauce, although I've altered it, using a vegetarian blue cheese sauce because that's one of our favourites. I've carried on doing fish which most of us like.'

ALL CHANGE!

The Kents were so impressed by the flavours and variety of their new food regime that when the week ended they decided to continue on a largely vegetarian diet.

But making the change wasn't all plain sailing. 'The big drawback is all the preparation involved,' says Sue. 'It takes much longer than before because of all the chopping.'

So do they feel healthier for their new eating habits? 'It's hard to say, but I think on the whole we do,' says Sue. 'I certainly experiment more with my cooking and use many more herbs and spices than I used to. I'm trying out lots of unusual vegetables that I wouldn't have tried before, such as okra. Vegetarian food is so interesting – it's opened my eyes to a whole new world of cooking!'

What's the overall verdict? Here's what each member of the Kent family had to say.

MICHAEL, 46

'I must say I have been quite impressed by some of the recipes Sue has prepared,' says Michael. 'I love curries and other spicy foods, and we have plenty of those. I reckon vegetable curry is every bit as good as meat curry. The one thing I do miss is the chewing you do with meat, something substantial to get your teeth into. If I was out to dinner I don't think I would refuse a steak. I do miss roast lamb but on the whole I think it has been a great success.'

JO, 16

Jo was the main driving force behind the family trying our plan – and the biggest convert, becoming a strict vegetarian after taking up our challenge.

'Jo used to eat chicken, but she doesn't touch meat or fish at all now,' says Sue. 'She doesn't even miss sausages!'

MARY, 81

Michael's mother was the most hesitant about vegetarianism, but nevertheless she tried everything and liked many of the dishes. However, she did find that too much vegetarian food can affect her digestion.

'It's been quite interesting but I wouldn't like to think I was never going to eat meat again,' she says. 'I prefer simpler, plain foods like egg and cheese or fish to the more exotic foods like okra and peppers. I've never liked herbs and spices either, and I'm not much of a pasta fan.'

SUE, 42

'I'd quite happily never eat meat again, although I'd find it hard to go without fish.'

ROBIN, 2

Robin currently eats fish but he doesn't really care for it so Sue expects he'll be a total vegetarian before long. 'Apart from that, he's not a fussy eater – on a good day he'll eat anything,' says Sue. 'He loves pasta, and vegetable soup goes down well.'

PAPER 2 WRITING (1 hour 30 minutes)

PART 1

*You **must** answer this question.*

1   You are a student at the Swansea College of Higher Education and are the
    secretary of the History Society. You have invited someone called Mr
    Stephens to speak to the Society, but have just realised that you won't be
    able to meet his train which arrives at 4.45. Your diary, a notice about his visit,
    and a map are shown below.

    Look at the diary, the notice and the map. Then write a letter to Mr Stephens
    using all the relevant information. Apologise for not being able to meet the train,
    explain why and suggest how he should get to the college from the station.

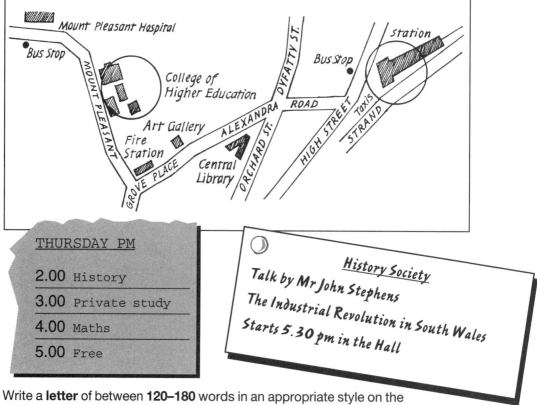

Write a **letter** of between **120–180** words in an appropriate style on the
opposite page. Do not write any addresses.

PART 1

PART 2

Write an answer to **one** *of the questions 2–5 in this part. Write your answer in* **120–180** *words in an appropriate style on the opposite page, putting the question number in the box.*

2   Your penfriend in Britain asks the following question in his or her latest letter:

> I'd like to try preparing a traditional dish from your country. Can you tell me how to do it?

Briefly **describe a typical dish** in your country and give instructions on how to prepare and serve it.

3   A local English-language paper runs a readers' column called **My big mistake**. Write a **story** for the column, describing the circumstances and effects of your mistake, and explaining why it happened.

4   Your teacher has asked you to write about two photographs from your family album which are of particular importance to you. **Describe** what the pictures show and what memories they bring back for you.

5   **Background reading texts**

Answer **one** of the following two questions based on your reading of **one** of the set books (see p. v). Write the title of the book next to the question number box.

Either **(a)**   Describe a moment which changes the course of the story and say why you think it is particularly important.

or **(b)**   Choose one of the important relationships in the book and describe how it develops.

PART 2

Question	

....

....

....

....

....

....

....

....

....

....

....

....

....

....

....

....

....

....

....

....

....

....

....

....

....

....

PAPER 3   USE OF ENGLISH (1 hour 15 minutes)

PART 1

For questions **1–15***, read the text below and decide which answer* **A, B, C** *or* **D**
best fits each space. There is an example at the beginning **(0)***.*
Mark your answers **on the separate answer sheet***.*

Example:
0   **A** descends   **B** falls   **C** drops   **D** jumps

0	A	B	C	D

ANGER ON THE ROADS

The anger that **(0)** .... on people when they get behind the steering wheel of a car
used to be **(1)** .... as a joke. But the laughter is getting noticeably quieter **(2)** .... that
the problem has become increasingly widespread.

(3) .... in a traffic jam, with family cars inching their **(4)** .... past, the driver of a fast
sports car begins to lose his temper. **(5)** .... the capabilities of his car, there is
nothing he can do. The **(6)** .... is anger.

Many people live in **(7)** .... of losing control. This is true of many situations but
driving is a good example. People think that the car might not start, it might break
(8) .... , or someone might run into it. Before anything even happens, people have
worked themselves up into a **(9)** .... of anxiety. And when something does happen,
they're **(10)** .... to explode. In fact, it's their very anxiety about losing control that
(11) .... them lose control.

This isn't to **(12)** .... that all offenders have psychological problems or drive
powerful sports cars. In fact, most of them are **(13)** .... ordinary human beings who
have no history of violence. There is **(14)** .... something deep in our nature that
(15) .... when we start up a car engine.

1 **A** found   **B** thought   **C** treated   **D** intended

2 **A** once   **B** even   **C** since   **D** now

3 **A** Set   **B** Stuck   **C** Held   **D** Fixed

4 **A** path   **B** way   **C** course   **D** route

5 **A** However   **B** Besides   **C** Although   **D** Despite

6 **A** outcome   **B** event   **C** issue   **D** effect

7 **A** worry   **B** fright   **C** fear   **D** concern

8 **A** up   **B** down   **C** out   **D** off

9 **A** state   **B** condition **C** feeling   **D** case

10 **A** good   **B** prepared   **C** near   **D** ready

11 **A** causes   **B** leads   **C** makes   **D** forces

12 **A** inform   **B** say   **C** tell   **D** announce

13 **A** purely   **B** fully   **C** exactly   **D** perfectly

14 **A** openly   **B** directly   **C** clearly   **D** frankly

15 **A** excites   **B** awakens   **C** disturbs   **D** upsets

---

PART 2

*For questions **16–30**, read the text below and think of the word which best fits each space. Use only **one** word in each space. There is an example at the beginning (**0**).*
*Write your word **on the separate answer sheet**.*

Example:

0	*to*	0

MISSION TO MARS

The Americans are keen to win the race **(0)** .... send human beings to Mars. In 1992, the new boss of NASA*, Dan Goldin, called on the American people to be the first to send explorers to **(16)** .... planet in the solar system. He reminded them **(17)** .... the symbolic gift carried to the moon and back by the Apollo 11 mission. It bears **(18)** .... message intended for the crew of the first spaceship to visit Mars. Goldin thinks **(19)** .... is time to begin the preparations **(20)** .... this historic journey. His speech echoed the words of the President, **(21)** ... promised that in 2019, 50 years after Neil Armstrong **(22)** .... the first man to set foot on the Moon, the first astronaut **(23)** .... stand on Mars.

(24) .... the end of the twentieth century, various unmanned spaceships will **(25)** .... thoroughly investigated the surface of the planet. But, however clever a robot **(26)** .... be, it cannot match the type of information **(27)** .... can be gained from direct human experience. The first geologist on the moon, Harrison Schmitt, was **(28)** .... of interpreting the story of the landscape on the spot. **(29)** .... humans walk on the red deserts of Mars, we will not be able to determine the history of this frozen world **(30)** .... any detail.

* The North American Space Agency

PART 3

*For questions **31–40**, complete the second sentence so that it has a similar meaning to the first sentence, using the word given.* **Do not change the word given.** *You must use between two and five words, including the word given. There is an example at the beginning (**0**).*
*Write **only** the missing words **on the separate answer sheet**.*

Example:

0 I last saw him at my 21st birthday party.
   since

   I .... my 21st birthday party.

The gap can be filled by the words 'haven't seen him since' so you write:

0	*haven't seen him since*	0	0 1 2

---

31 'Why don't you wait by the phone box, Brenda?' said Leslie.
   Brenda

   Leslie suggested .... by the phone box.

32 Although he overslept, Clive wasn't late for work.
   up

   Despite .... on time, Clive wasn't late for work.

33 I haven't eaten food like this before.
   time

   This is the .... this sort of food.

34 After a long chase, the police finally succeeded in arresting the thief.
   to

   After a long chase, the police finally .... the thief.

35 Diane was supposed to write to her parents last week.
   ought

   Diane .... to her parents last week.

36 His handwriting is so small I can hardly read it.
such

He .... I can hardly read it.

37 Somebody has to pick the visitors up from the airport.
up

The visitors .... from the airport.

38 I wish I hadn't told him what we were planning to do this evening.
regret

I .... for this evening.

39 Everyone was surprised to see Geoff leave the party early.
surprise

To .... the party early.

40 All the witnesses said the accident was my fault.
blame

All the witnesses said that .... the accident.

PART 4

*For questions **41–55**, read the text below and look carefully at each line. Some of the lines are correct, and some have a word which should not be there. If a line is correct, put a tick (✓) by the number **on the separate answer sheet**. If a line has a word which should **not** be there, write the word **on the separate answer sheet**. There are two examples at the beginning (**0** and **00**).*

Examples:

 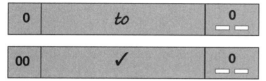

| 0 | to | 0 |
| 00 | ✓ | 0 |

A MUCH-IMPROVED JOURNEY

0	Shortly after reaching to Weymouth on the south coast of England
00	on holiday, we caught sight of a small white dot on the horizon,
41	moving at an amazing speed. Surely it couldn't be a ship going so
42	fast? We thought it might still be a trick of the light, but as the shape
43	came closer, it was clear so that we had not been mistaken: it was
44	indeed some sort of a ship and it was travelling very much faster
45	than a normal boat could ever have done in similar conditions.
46	It turned out as to be the new high-speed ferry to the Channel
47	Islands, which could reach Guernsey in just over the two hours. This
48	seemed incredible since the last time when we had visited the island,
49	it had taken us for five hours to get there, but now, with this faster
50	service, a day trip it was clearly a real possibility and we decided to
51	buy tickets for the next day. It also meant getting to the harbour by six
52	o'clock but it was certainly worth making the effort to get up early.
53	The weather was fine and the ferry lived well up to its claims for a
54	comfortable crossing. By half past nine we were relaxing ourselves in
55	a Guernsey café, enjoying a leisurely breakfast and looking out across
	the sea.

PART 5

*For questions **56–65**, read the text below. Use the word given in capitals at the end of each line to form a word that fits in the space in the same line. There is an example at the beginning (**0**). Write your word **on the separate answer sheet**.*

Example:

0	*marvellous*	0

THE ABC OF COOKING

It's a **(0)** .... idea for children to do some cooking at an early   **MARVEL**
age. Generally **(56)** .... , most children can't wait to help in the   **SPEAK**
kitchen and love getting involved in the **(57)** .... of their meals.   **PREPARE**
They should be **(58)** .... to do so, and care should be taken to   **COURAGE**
(59) .... they enjoy the experience. It is important to show them   **SURE**
how to do things **(60)** .... but they shouldn't be criticised too much.   **CORRECT**
Although the finished result may not be quite to your **(61)** .... , the   **LIKE**
young cook will undoubtedly find it quite the **(62)** .... food he or   **TASTY**
she has ever eaten.

Kitchens can, of course, be **(63)** .... places and so the absolute   **DANGER**
(64) .... of keeping an eye on children at all times cannot be   **IMPORTANT**
emphasised too **(65)** .... . Sharp knives, for example, should be   **HEAVY**
avoided until children are old enough to handle them safely.

PAPER 4   LISTENING (approximately 40 minutes)

PART 1

You will hear people talking in eight different situations.
*For questions **1–8**, choose the best answer **A**, **B** or **C**.*

1   These women are talking about a colleague.
What do they feel about his behaviour?

   A   It was typical of him.

   B   It had improved.

   C   It reminded them of someone else.

               1

2   This man is talking about a sports event.
What happened to his team?

   A   They won.

   B   They did better than he'd hoped.

   C   They were very unlucky.

               2

3   Listen to this man telephoning someone about his washing machine.
Who is he talking to?

   A   an engineer

   B   a friend

   C   the shop he bought it from

               3

4   You switch on the radio and hear this report.
Where is it coming from?

   A   a market

   B   a concert hall

   C   a racetrack

               4

5 You hear this man talking about his bad back.
How did he injure it?

   A in a road accident

   B by lifting something

   C in a fight

	5

6 You overhear these people talking about a book.
What sort of book is it?

   A a guidebook

   B a history book

   C a novel

	6

7 Listen to this woman who has just arrived at a meeting.
Why is she late?

   A The weather was bad.

   B There was a traffic jam.

   C She crashed her car.

	7

8 At the sports club you hear these people discussing an exercise.
What is its purpose?

   A to help you lose weight

   B to make you relax

   C to strengthen the stomach muscles

	8

PART 2

You will hear part of a radio programme about holidays.
For questions 9–18, complete the grid.

	Eastingham	Brant	Faresey
Main attraction	9	13	16
Size	10	14	
Best transport to get there	11	15	17
Best time of year	12		18

PART 3

You will hear five people talking about clothes.
*For questions **19–23**, choose from the list **A–F** what each speaker is talking about.*
Use the letters only once. There is one extra letter which you do not need to use.

A   a hat

B   a shirt

Speaker 1	**19**

C   an overcoat

Speaker 2	**20**

Speaker 3	**21**

D   a suit

Speaker 4	**22**

E   a sock

Speaker 5	**23**

F   a boot

PART 4

You will hear two friends discussing evening study courses.
For questions 24–30, decide which course each statement refers to.

Mark   **A** *for Art*
     or   **C** *for Computers*
     or   **S** *for Spanish*

24   You must book a place on this course.   **24**

25   Polly already knows this subject.   **25**

26   This course is taught by a qualified teacher.   **26**

27   There's an extra charge for this course.   **27**

28   This course lasts for two terms.   **28**

29   Students work hard on this course.   **29**

30   Polly would do this course if she had time.   **30**

PAPER 5   SPEAKING (14 minutes)

Part 1

You tell the examiner about yourself. The examiner may ask you questions such as: Where are you from? How do you usually spend your free time? What are your plans for the future? Your partner does the same.

Part 2

The examiner gives you two pictures to look at and asks you to talk about them for about a minute. Your partner does the same with two different pictures.

Part 3

The examiner gives you a photograph or drawing to look at with your partner. You are asked to solve a problem or come to a decision about something in the picture. For example, you might be asked to decide the best way to use some rooms in a language school. You discuss the problem together.

Part 4

You are asked more questions connected with your discussion in Part 3. For example, you might be asked to talk about the best ways of studying.

Book 2 contents

Thanks

We are grateful to Jeanne McCarten, Elizabeth Sharman, Amanda Ogden, Judith Greet and Peter Ducker of CUP for their hard work in helping us; to everyone at AVP Recording Studio and to all the people at UCLES who provided us with information.

The authors and publishers would also like to thank the following people and institutions for piloting the material for us:

International House, Zaragoza; The Cheltenham School of English; Anna Bogobowicz, Warsaw; Eurocentres, Cambridge; The William Blake Institute, Buenos Aires.

Acknowledgements

The publishers are grateful to the following for permission to reproduce copyright material. It has not always been possible to identify sources of all the material used, and in such cases the publishers would welcome information from the copyright owners.

Focus magazine for the extracts on p.5 (*Focus* March 1995), on pp.36-37 (*Focus* July 1994), on pp.94-95 (*Focus* July 1994) and on p.24 (*Focus* May 1993); *The Observer* for the extract on pp.6-7 from 'The Summit of Self-Made Satisfaction' by Roger Smith (*The Observer* 30.5.96); *BBC Music Magazine* for the extract on pp.9-10 from 'Bell Epoque' by Lindsay Kemp (*BBC Music Magazine* December 1993); *National Magazine Company* for the extract on p.13 from 'Do women do it better?' by Gillian Fairchild (*Good Housekeeping* March 1993) and for the extract on p.67 from 'Guide to the guides' by James Daunt (*Country Living Traveller* February 1995); *The Radio Times* for the extract on pp.32-33 from 'My kind of day' by Colin Jackson (*Radio Times* 20-26 August 1994) and for the extract on pp.87-88 from 'Take One Novice' (*Radio Times* 10-16 September 1994); Nicola Upson for the extracts on pp.34-35 from 'Learning to play the piano' by Charlotte Cory (*Second Shift* Issue 4) and on pp.60-61 from 'Biologically correct' by Heather Angel (*Second Shift* Issue 4); *Mediawatch Ltd* for the extract on p.39 (*Healthy Eating* March 1994); the extract on pp.58-59 is from *Which?* December 1991, published by Consumer's Association, 2 Marylebone Road, London NW1 4DF. To find out more, including how to get *Which?* free for 3 months, please write to Department A3, FREEPOST, Hertford SG14 1YB or telephone free on 0800 252100; *Financial Times* for the extract on pp.63-64 (*Financial Times* 19/20.11.94); *The Guardian* for the extract on p.86 from 'Unable to think about it' (*Education Guardian* 18.1.94); the extract on pp.90-91 is from the World-Wide Research and Publishing Company's 'National Parkways, Yosemite National Park'; Jean Saunders and Donna Thompson for the extract on p.20 adapted from 'How to write a bestseller' (*Woman's Weekly* 30.8.94); *Wildlife Magazine* for the extract on p.44 adapted from 'The whatsit of Oz' by Richard Greenwell (*Wildlife Magazine* February 1994); *Kogan Page* Publishers for the extract on p.50 adapted from *Job Hunting for Women* (2nd ed.) by Margaret Wallis, published 1990 by *Kogan Page Ltd*, London; *IPC Magazines* for the extract on p.74 adapted from 'We're on the box – again!' by Nuala Duxbury (*Woman's Realm* 23.8.94); *Reed Books* for the extract on p.78 adapted from *The World of Toys* by J Kandert (Octopus Illustrated Publishing); *Element Books Ltd* of Shaftesbury, Dorset for the extract on p.100 adapted from *The Elements of Visualisation* by Ursula Markham (*Element Books* 1989); Ray K. Kinross for the extract on p.102 adapted from 'Ice rage after ice age' by Felicity Kinross (*The Times Saturday Review* 17.8.1991); *Popular Crafts* Magazine for the extract on p.106 adapted from 'Making a living' (*Popular Crafts* April 1994); the answer sheets for Papers 1, 3 and 4 are reproduced by permission of the *University of Cambridge Local Examinations Syndicate*.

Photographs: Action-Plus/Tony Henshaw, p.32; Heather Angel, p.60; Harry Borden, p.9; Comstock Photo Library, p.90; Country Living/Wong Ling, p.67; Financial Times Pictures, p.63; The Hulton Deutsch Collection, p.58; Pictor International-London, p.36; Rex Features Ltd, pp.87, 94; Tony Stone Images/Philip and Karen Smith, p.6.

Colour Paper 5 Section: Adams Picture Library (2C); Gainsborough: Wooded Landscape, Christies, London/Bridgeman Art Library, London (1A); British Telecommunications plc (2E: telephone); The J. Allan Cash Photolibrary (3E: bottom left); The Environmental Picture Library Ltd/Graham Burns (3E: top right); Chris Fairclough Colour Library (3E: middle left); Hitachi Home Electronics (Europe) Ltd (2E: television, radio-cassette player); Jeremy Pembrey (1D, 2E: armchair, computer, bookshelves, 4E: top right, bottom); Performing Arts Library/Clive Barda (4A); Pictor-International-London (3C, 4D); Redferns/Mick Hutson (4B); Beth Gwinn/Retna Pictures Ltd (4C); Tony Stone Images (3D); Topham Picturepoint (2A); Trip/Helene Rogers (2D); Viewfinder Colour Photo Library (2B, 3A); John Walmsley Photo Library (3B, 4E: top left); Painting 'Shining Stream of Time' (1994) by Julius Tabacek (1B); Computer Art 'Life Study' (1992) by Abbas Hashemi (1C); Architect's plan by Peter Byatt (1E).

Picture research by Sandie Huskison-Rolfe (PHOTOSEEKERS)

Book design by Peter Ducker MSTD

Practice Test 1

PAPER 1 READING (1 hour 15 minutes)

*You are going to read a magazine article about air pollution. Choose from the list (**A–H**) the sentence which best summarises each part (**1–6**) of the article. There is an extra sentence which you do not need to use. There is an example at the beginning (**0**).*

*Mark your answers **on the separate answer sheet**.*

A	Research is being done into electric cars.
B	People refuse to give up their cars in cities.
C	One answer is to persuade people to buy electric cars.
D	Cities where people depend heavily on cars have the worst problems.
E	Electric cars have a major disadvantage.
F	Air pollution appears to be a cause of illness.
G	Air pollution is now a worry for everyone.
H	Cars are destroying the air quality in cities.

Cars switch on to plugged-in power

0	*H*

Around the world, governments and their citizens are becoming increasingly concerned about what the motor car and its internal combustion engine do to the air we breathe. In some cities, air pollution resulting from the internal combustion engine is so bad that drastic action has had to be taken. In summertime, pollution in some southern European cities is now so serious that it is common for half the usual number of commuters to be forbidden to bring their cars into the city.

1	

Calculating the number of people who become unwell or even die as a result of air pollution is very difficult. But recent studies of the effects of car fumes suggest that the health risks may be more severe than previously thought.

2	

Suddenly, urban air pollution is no longer a subject just for environmentalists but a cause of widespread public concern. Ordinary people are beginning to sit up and take notice.

3	

There are numerous proposed ways of dealing with the problem: one of the most radical is to slowly stop using the internal combustion engine and to use instead the electric motor powered from a large battery pack. A lot of money is now being invested by car and battery manufacturers to create 'clean' vehicles.

4	

Much of the pressure has come from the land where the car is king – California. The United States has no public transport to speak of (the major car-makers actively contributed to its destruction) so the car is the average American's only practical means of daily transport. But some US cities, Los Angeles in particular, are paying a high price for this over-reliance. LA's famous smogs – trapped by the natural 'bowl' of the nearby mountains – are the result of reactions between the chemicals which come from the city's millions of car exhausts.

5	

Because of this serious pollution problem, California has for over 20 years set tough pollution laws. Even so, LA's smog problem has not been solved. So now, the 'sunshine state' has taken the first step towards removing the internal combustion engine altogether from its roads. From 1998, all car-makers who sell their cars in California will have to offer a proportion of electric cars for sale. In 1998 the proportion of electric cars offered must be two per cent, rising to five per cent by 2003 and to ten per cent by 2005.

6	

Environmentalists argue, with some justification, that only by making laws like this can politicians force change on the car industry. But others – some of them no less committed to cleaner urban air – doubt that the totally electric car is the right solution to the problem. The difficulty with electric cars is that they can only travel a short distance at a time. At the moment there is no obvious solution to the transport problems of the world's cities.

PART 2

You are going to read a newspaper article about backpacking. For questions
7–14, *choose the answer (**A**, **B**, **C** or **D**) which you think fits best according to the*
text.
Mark your answers **on the separate answer sheet**.

Self-made satisfaction

IT HAD been a long, hard, wonderful day. The two of us had walked from the sea's edge through the length of a beautiful valley, climbed a superb mountain, traversed its narrow, rocky ridge, and now stood on its final peak, tired, happy and looking for the perfect camp site.

The experienced backpacker has a natural feeling for such things, and our eyes were drawn to a small blue circle on the map, like an eye winking at us. We could not see it from where we were, but we followed our judgement and descended steeply until it came into view.

We were right. It was a calm pool, with flat grass beside it. Gently taking our packs off, we made the first of many cups of tea before putting up our tent. Later that evening, over another cup of tea and after a good meal, we sat outside the tent watching the sun set over a glittering sea dotted with islands, towards one of which a ferry was slowly moving. It is not always so perfect, of course. On another trip, with a different companion, a thoroughly wet day had ended at a lonely farm. Depressed at the thought of camping, we had knocked and asked if we could use a barn as a shelter.

Backpacking could be defined as the art of

comfortable, self-sufficient travel on foot. Everything you need is in the pack on your back, and you become emotionally as well as physically attached to it. I once left my pack hidden in some rocks while I made a long trip to a peak I particularly wanted to climb. I was away for nearly three hours and ended up running the last stretch in fear that my precious pack would not be there. It was, of course.

The speed at which the backpacker travels makes this the perfect way to see any country. You experience the landscape as a slow unfolding scene, almost in the way it was made; and you find time to stop and talk to people you meet. I've learned much local history from simply chatting to people met while walking through an area. At the end of a trip, whether three days or three weeks, there's a good feeling of achievement, of having got somewhere under your own power.

After years of going out walking just for the day, many people start backpacking simply through wanting to stay out rather than cut short a trip.

In Britain, the backpacker is necessarily restricted and directed to a degree. There are no areas completely untouched by humans, though we do have fine wild country. In the north-west of Scotland, I have managed to walk for three days without crossing a road or passing an inhabited house. In the lowlands, your overnight stops may have to be on recognised camp sites. In upland country, you have the priceless gift of choosing where to camp. Even here, many factors come into play, and I shan't easily forget a night camped on a ski run surrounded by fences: we were simply too tired to go any further.

There is one important rule the good backpacker should follow: respect the land and its people – as the Americans say, 'take only photographs (one might add memories), leave only footprints'.

With good equipment, you can survive just about anything the weather can throw at you – and modern equipment is very good indeed. Of course, you need to know how to use it – go to a specialist outdoor shop for good advice. In particular, you need to be confident in map reading.

As with any other sport, start gently and locally, improve your skills and gradually widen your horizons. Britain is only crowded in patches and there is still plenty of space for the backpacker wanting to be alone.

7   The writer and his companion knew there was a pool because
   A   they had seen it earlier in the day.
   B   they had been told about it.
   C   they could see it on the map.
   D   they could see it from the top of the mountain.

8   What does 'it' refer to in line 13?
   A   the pool
   B   the mountain
   C   the camp site
   D   the map

9   How did they feel at the end of the day?
   A   They wished they could have found a farm.
   B   They were delighted with the spot they'd found.
   C   They were anxious about the weather to come.
   D   They were too tired to put up their tent.

10 What does the writer mean by being 'emotionally as well as physically attached' to his backpack (lines 31–32)?
    A He might die on the mountains without it.
    B It is not a good idea to leave it anywhere.
    C He walks better when he is wearing it.
    D It is more than just a practical aid.

11 According to the writer, the main advantage of backpacking is that you can
    A find out how the landscape was made.
    B gain an understanding of the area you walk through.
    C make new friends while walking.
    D get fitter as you walk.

12 What does the writer mean by 'the priceless gift of choosing where to camp' (lines 63–64)?
    A It is not usually possible to camp wherever you want.
    B Camp sites are often quite expensive.
    C Some of the camp sites are difficult to reach.
    D Some areas do not have suitable camp sites for backpackers.

13 What advice does the writer give about backpacking?
    A You should take lots of photographs to remind you of your trip.
    B You should avoid spending too much on equipment.
    C You should first walk in an area you are familiar with.
    D You should only go out in suitable weather.

14 What difference between backpacking and walking does the writer mention?
    A Backpackers travel in pairs or groups.
    B Backpackers never sleep indoors.
    C Backpackers' routes are carefully planned.
    D Backpackers' walks last longer than a day.

PART 3

*You are going to read a magazine article about a violinist. Seven paragraphs have been removed from the article. Choose from the paragraphs (**A–H**) the one which fits each gap (**15–20**). There is one extra paragraph which you do not need to use. There is an example at the beginning (**0**).*

*Mark your answers **on the separate answer sheet**.*

Where's the Festival Hall?

'Where's the Festival Hall from here?' The question leaves me a little surprised. Joshua Bell and I are gazing out from his room in London's Savoy Hotel – straight at the Festival Hall, in fact. Cautiously, I point out the building, but little surprise registers on his much-photographed face. Perhaps it's the jet lag.

0	*H*

'Actually, I think I manage touring better than many,' he declares. 'It doesn't really bother me, because I happen to like going to new places and I love hotels. I don't even mind long transatlantic flights. At this point it's still exciting for me.' He does need to escape every so often though, and I had already found this out.

15	

He apologises: 'I'd been on the road and realised I had four complete full days off. I think I was in Scotland and had to be in Cologne five days later. I felt like I just needed to get home, so I hopped on a plane.'

16	

'My teacher, Josef Gingold, encouraged me to perform as much as I could, to get out there and do it. I think the fact that I was so young then and on stage might be one of the reasons why I feel comfortable on stage now. I don't feel like it's something foreign. I feel that's where I can do my best work, and so I don't get anxious or anything like that.'

17	

'It was the first time I'd played with a major orchestra, and I clearly remember the feeling of hearing such a polished sound; I was just blown away by it.'

18	

Three years after that, Bell made his first tour to Europe with the St Louis Symphony Orchestra, and his first London performance happened the following year. And it was around then, too, that he began to make a lot of appearances in

the advertising pages of the music press.

19	

Did he think such publicity was damaging? 'Well, not in the long run. In the end, people will judge me for what I do, and if they don't like me for that, that's fine. I would hate for someone to judge me just on what they think of record companies. I heard of several critics who said they wouldn't even listen to my records.'

20	

Bell has indeed outlived that image. His playing has consistently drawn praise for its effortless mastery and beautiful tone.

A After nine years of doing concert tours, Bell knows when he needs a break. He feels the early start to his career was very useful.

B What did he think of that? 'It was unfortunate, but it's been several years since then. And people in the music world did get to know who I was in a fairly short time. But it's only now that I've stopped hearing about it, even in the good reviews.'

C Bell also remembers the warmth shown him by the members of the orchestra: 'At that time I was the youngest ever to have played in a subscription concert there. They heard I collected coins and several of the players gave me things from their own collections. It was a nice feeling.'

D This is my second attempt at meeting the fresh-faced American violinist: I remind him that, a few weeks earlier, the first attempt failed because of his sudden decision to fly home to New York.

E 'It's unfortunate that most instrumentalists today don't write their own music. In the old days everybody did. I've no idea if I'd be successful at writing music, but it's something I'd love to do.'

F He now admits to feeling uncomfortable about the boy-next-door image his record company seemed eager to present at that time, especially in the light of the reaction it caused in Britain, where he was not as well-known as he was back home in the States.

G There were no nerves, according to Bell, when at 14 he did his first professional concerto performance with the Philadelphia Orchestra. Naturally, though, the occasion made a lasting impression.

H Throughout our interview, Bell yawns and rubs his eyes. I begin to feel bad about not letting him sleep.

PART 4

You are going to read a magazine article about women writers. For questions
21–35, *choose from the people (**A–E**). Some of the people may be chosen more
than once. When more than one answer is required, these may be given in any
order. There is an example at the beginning (**0**).*
Mark your answers **on the separate answer sheet**.

A	Gill Coleridge
B	Margaret Drabble
C	Margaret Forster
D	Frances Fyfield
E	Ruth Rendell

Which woman makes the following statement?

Male and female authors do not write in the same way.	**0**	*B*	
Women's attitudes to life are reflected in today's fiction.	**21**		
Men could profit from reading novels written by women.	**22**		
She does not aim her writing at men or women in particular.	**23**		**24**
Authors write about things they feel comfortable with.	**25**		
You can't always guess whether a book is by a man or a woman.	**26**		
Fiction written for men tends to have a strong storyline.	**27**		
An equal number of men and women react to her books.	**28**		
Some women have been her fans for a long time.	**29**		

She aims her writing mainly at women.

30	

She doesn't change her writing because of what other people might think.

31	

Women readers like to get emotionally involved with the characters in a novel.

32	

Her main aim is for her books to be interesting.

33	

Authors who want financial success aim at a particular type of reader.

34	

Women like reading about other women who lead more fulfilled lives.

35	

Is what we believe about women writers fact or fiction?

Women read more than men: that's official. And statistically, what do they like reading best? Novels. Novels about love, novels about crime, novels that are funny, clever and deep but above all, novels written by other women.

There is, of course, an enormous difference between 'popular' and 'literary' fiction. As literary agent **Gill Coleridge** explains, 'In the commercial side of the business, the most important feature of male fiction is the plot, whereas in female fiction it is characters that the reader can identify with and care about. Commercial authors focus on a chosen audience, writers of literary novels write what they want to say.'

Margaret Drabble, who has written several successful literary novels, says that she never imagines her reader to be male or female when she sits down to write. 'That person changes from chapter to chapter. Sometimes I think about friends – I bet Judith would like this or James would hate that, but it doesn't affect what I write. There's

been a change in the last two or three decades in how a whole generation of women look at the world and therefore what they accept in their fiction. Luckily for me, a fairly loyal readership of women has grown old along with me, taken the same journey. But because men and women react differently to things, there is a difference in how male and female authors write. We tend to write about things we like and which are sympathetic to us.' She claims to be much more aware now of the male reader, because the different worlds which men and women live in are less separate nowadays than they used to be.

As a novelist and biographer (she has written the life stories of several well-known people), **Margaret Forster** says of the letters she receives from readers that men and women write to her in equal numbers. Of women readers she says, 'Women are hungry for details of other people's lives, particularly women's lives: biography as well as fiction provides that second-hand

experience. Many women get to middle age and wonder where their life has gone, why they haven't made more of it: reading about others who have achieved something enlarges their vision.'

Crime writer **Frances Fyfield** wishes that more men would read more fiction, especially by women. 'If all you read is thrillers and adventures, you're bound to have a gap of knowledge. I write very much with the female reader in mind, though I take my male readers into account too.'

Crime writer **Ruth Rendell** says she cannot always tell male writing from female writing: 'Women are always credited with being better at writing detail, men with taking the wider view. But I've just been rereading Anthony Powell's *A Dance To The Music Of Time* and it's full of detail. Just as many men as women read my books. I don't think of my audience as being one or the other, only that there shouldn't be too many things that they find dull.'

PAPER 2 WRITING (1 hour 30 minutes)

PART 1

*You **must** answer this question.*

1   You have received a letter from a friend, asking for information about a
    swimming course you attended last year.

> By the way, my brother is thinking of taking his family on
> a swimming course this summer. He and his wife are serious
> swimmers, but their children are very young and can't swim yet
> so they're looking for somewhere with plenty of variety. Did
> you have a good time when you went to Merle Park? I seem to
> remember you had a few problems.
>
>   Could you let me know what you thought of the place, and
> whether you think they would enjoy it? Thanks.
>
> Best wishes
>
> *Stephen*

Read the letter carefully, and look at the leaflet from last year's courses, on
which you have written some notes. Then write to your friend, answering his
questions and explaining whether this course would be suitable or not.

Write a **letter** of between **120–180** words in an appropriate style on the next
page. Do not write any addresses.

PART 1

....

....

....

....

....

....

....

....

....

....

....

....

....

....

....

....

....

....

....

....

....

....

....

....

....

....

....

PART 2

*Write an answer to **one** of the questions **2–5** in this part. Write your answer in*
120–180 *words in an appropriate style on the next page, putting the question*
number in the box.

2

—— Sunrise Travel ——
announce their
Summer Fun Competition.

Three lucky winners will receive two weeks' holiday, all
expenses paid, at a destination of their choice.

To take part, all you have to do is describe the best or worst
holiday you have ever had.

Write your **description** for the travel company's competition.

3 A student magazine has asked readers to send in short stories which include
the sentence: **All at once I began to understand why I was being treated
so well**.

Write your **story**.

4 Your local tourist information office is putting together a leaflet for visitors.
You have been asked to write a report on shopping facilities in your area.

Write your **report**.

5 **Background reading texts**

Answer **one** of the following two questions based on your reading of **one** of
the set books (see p. v). Write the title of the book next to the question
number box.

Either **(a)** Describe the events which lead up to the most important
moment in the story.

or **(b)** Describe some of the most important people in the book and
explain how they affect the story.

PART 2

Question	

....

....

....

....

....

....

....

....

....

....

....

....

....

....

....

....

....

....

....

....

....

....

....

....

....

....

....

PAPER 3   USE OF ENGLISH (1 hour 15 minutes)

PART 1

*For questions **1–15**, read the text below and decide which answer **A**, **B**, **C** or **D**
best fits each space. There is an example at the beginning (**0**).
Mark your answers **on the separate answer sheet**.*

Example:

0   **A** ever   **B** once   **C** only   **D** never

0	A	B	C	D
	▬	▭	▭	▭

FAMILY HISTORY

In an age when technology is developing faster than (**0**) .... before, many people are
being (**1**) .... to the idea of looking back into the past. One way they can do this is by
investigating their own family history. They can try to (**2**) .... out more about where
their families came from and what they did. This is now a fast-growing hobby,
especially in countries with a (**3**) .... short history, like Australia and the United States.

It is (**4**) .... thing to spend some time (**5**) .... through a book on family history and to
take the (**6**) .... to investigate your own family's past. It is (**7**) .... another to carry out
the research work successfully. It is easy to set about it in a disorganised way and
(**8**) .... yourself many problems which could have been (**9**) .... with a little forward
planning.

If your own family stories tell you that you are (**10**) .... with a famous character,
whether hero or criminal, do not let this idea take over your research. Just (**11**) .... it
as an interesting possibility. A simple system (**12**) .... collecting and storing your
information will be adequate to start with; a more complex one may only get in your
(**13**) .... . The most important thing, though, is to (**14**) .... started. Who knows what
you (**15**) .... find?

1   **A** pushed   **B** attracted   **C** fetched   **D** brought

2   **A** lay   **B** make   **C** put   **D** find

3   **A** fairly   **B** greatly   **C** mostly   **D** widely

4   **A** a   **B** one   **C** no   **D** some

5   **A** seeing   **B** moving   **C** going   **D** living

6   **A** idea   **B** plan   **C** purpose   **D** decision

7   **A** quite   **B** just   **C** more   **D** even

8   **A** produce   **B** cause   **C** build   **D** create

9   **A** missed   **B** lost   **C** avoided   **D** escaped

10 **A** connected   **B** joined   **C** attached   **D** related

11 **A** treat   **B** control   **C** contact   **D** direct

12 **A** with   **B** by   **C** for   **D** through

13 **A** track   **B** path   **C** road   **D** way

14 **A** get   **B** appear   **C** be   **D** feel

15 **A** should   **B** might   **C** ought   **D** must

PART 2

For questions **16–30**, *read the text below and think of the word which best fits each space. Use only* **one** *word in each space. There is an example at the beginning* (**0**).

Write your word **on the separate answer sheet**.

Example: | **0** | *to* | | **0** |

WRITING A STORY

Where do you start if you want **(0)** .... write a successful story? Clearly, what you need first of **(16)** .... is an idea which you can develop into a strong plot. But **(17)** .... do ideas like this come from? The **(18)** .... is 'anywhere and everywhere'. They may come from something that has **(19)** .... to you or to **(20)** .... else, from a newspaper, an interesting picture, or even a song. It's a good idea to keep a notebook nearby **(21)** .... that you can write down the details of any odd incidents **(22)** .... catch your imagination. Make a note of ideas **(23)** .... titles too, and any special phrases or descriptions that you think of. A small tape recorder can **(24)** .... useful for this purpose. Some writers even keep **(25)** .... by their bed in **(26)** .... they wake up with the 'idea of the century'.

Another method of developing the story is to make use **(27)** .... the characters themselves. Why not **(28)** .... putting three people you know well into a situation such as a wedding, where feelings may be very strong, and see **(29)** .... happens. But don't make the final characters too much like your Aunt Jane or Uncle Jim or you may find **(30)** .... in real trouble.

PART 3

*For questions **31–40**, complete the second sentence so that it has a similar meaning to the first sentence, using the word given. **Do not change the word given**. You must use between two and five words, including the word given. There is an example at the beginning (**0**).*
*Write **only** the missing words **on the separate answer sheet**.*

Example:

0   The tennis star ignored her coach's advice.
   attention

   The tennis star didn't .... her coach's advice.

The gap can be filled by the words 'pay any attention to' so you write:

0	*pay any attention to*		0	0 1 2

---

31   No one has explained why our flight is delayed.
   reason

   No one has .... the delay to our flight.

32   I'd rather you didn't phone me at work.
   prefer

   I'd .... me at work.

33   When Mary wanted a new car, she had to save up for a year.
   Mary

   It .... save up to buy a new car.

34   They are letting David out of hospital next week.
   released

   David .... hospital next week.

35   'Did you leave a tip for the waiter, Dad?' I asked.
   he

   I asked my father .... a tip for the waiter.

36 Jane didn't expect to win the competition, but she entered it anyway.
  went

  Jane didn't expect to win the competition, but she .... it anyway.

37 I do not intend to tell you my plans.
  intention

  I .... you my plans.

38 Don't sign for the parcel until you have checked that everything is there.
  you

  Make sure that nothing is .... sign for the parcel.

39 Sasha only moved to a new class because her teacher recommended it.
  Sasha

  If her teacher hadn't recommended it, ... to a new class.

40 The motor in this machine needs cleaning once a week.
  has

  The motor in this machine .... once a week.

PART 4

For questions **41–55**, read the text below and look carefully at each line. Some of the lines are correct, and some have a word which should not be there. If a line is correct, put a tick (✓) by the number **on the separate answer sheet**. If a line has a word which should **not** be there, write the word **on the separate answer sheet**. There are two examples at the beginning (**0** and **00**).

Examples:

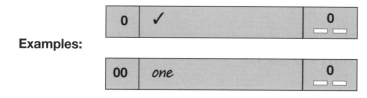

A FAULTY PURCHASE

Dear Sir

0	I am writing to complain about the condition of the cassette
00	recorder which one I bought from your shop on Tuesday,
41	3rd March. Although the outer box it was in perfect
42	condition, I found when I arrived home that the player by
43	itself had obviously been used before and had the
44	several scratches on its case. The headphone cable was
45	badly twisted and I do not think so it will be long before the
46	headphones themselves go out of their shape altogether.
47	In addition, neither of the two free cassettes which came
48	up with the machine was at the beginning. I am sure they
49	must have been being played before by a previous customer,
50	or perhaps the machine had then been used for demonstration
51	purposes. Since there is nothing wrong with the sound quality
52	of the player, but, as I had paid full price, I have a right to expect
53	to receive a brand new equipment. I would therefore be grateful
54	if you would replace for the player with a new model of the
55	same type. I look forward to hearing from you in due course.

Yours faithfully

PART 5

*For questions **56–65**, read the text below. Use the word given in capitals at the end of each line to form a word that fits in the space in the same line. There is an example at the beginning (**0**). Write your word **on the separate answer sheet**.*

Example: | 0 | *outer* | 0 __ __ |

LIFE ON OTHER PLANETS

Humans have long been fascinated by **(0)** …. space, and have   **OUT**
wondered if there are intelligent life-forms **(56)** …. , which we might   **ELSE**
be able to contact. **(57)** …. , we've all seen space creatures on our   **NATURE**
TV and cinema screens, but 'aliens' like these owe more to the **(58)** …. **CONVENIENT**
of using human **(59)** …. to play the parts than to any real form of   **ACT**
(60) …. investigation.   **SCIENCE**

However, many serious space **(61)** …. are now beginning to turn their   **RESEARCH**
attention to the question of what alien life might **(62)** …. look like. One **ACTUAL**
early result is Arnold the Alien, **(63)** …. by biologist, Dougal Dixon. This **DESIGN**
strange being, **(64)** …. humans, has its eyes, ears and limbs in groups   **LIKE**
of three instead of pairs but, despite its odd **(65)** …. , its behaviour is **APPEAR**
not very different from our own.

PAPER 4 LISTENING (approximately 40 minutes)

PART 1

You will hear people talking in eight different situations.
*For questions **1–8**, choose the best answer **A**, **B** or **C**.*

1 You hear someone introducing a programme on the radio.
 Where is he?

 A a swimming pool

 B a sports hall

 C a football ground

 ```
 [    | 1 ]
 ```

2 You hear this girl talking to her mother.
 What plan had her mother agreed to?

 A visiting a friend

 B going to London

 C staying in a hotel

 ```
 [    | 2 ]
 ```

3 You hear this advertisement for a concert.
 What is unusual about it?

 A It's on a Saturday.

 B It's in a different place.

 C There will be singers in it.

 ```
 [    | 3 ]
 ```

4 You hear this woman talking about herself.
 What does she feel?

 A regret

 B pride

 C satisfaction

 ```
 [    | 4 ]
 ```

5 Listen to this man on the phone.
Why is he calling?

    A to apologise for being late

    B to report escaped animals

    C to offer his help

6 You hear this reporter on the television.
Who is he going to talk to?

    A a businessman

    B a politician

    C a shopper

7 This boy is talking about something he's been working on.
What is it?

    A a garden

    B a water sports centre

    C a nature reserve

8 You hear this woman talking to someone outside a block of flats.
What is her job?

    A She sells property.

    B She is a tourist guide.

    C She inspects building work.

PART 2

You will hear two radio presenters talking about some of the programmes for the coming month.
For questions 9–18, complete the information. You will need to write a word or a short phrase.

Monday 6th
Elton John talking about his

	9

Wednesday 8th
Win a prize by guessing name of the

	10

Thursday 9th
Sez U's visit to

	11

Friday 17th
Report from US on lifestyle of

	12

Monday 20th
How to save money by using

	13

Friday 24th
Programme about children of former

	14

Monday 27th
Music from

	15

Competition prize

	16

Tuesday 28th
Report from

	17

Wednesday 29th
New fashions for people who go

	18

PART 3

You will hear five people talking about the jobs they'd like to have.
*For questions **19–23**, choose from the list **A–F** what they describe. Use the letters*
only once. There is one extra letter which you do not need to use.

This person would like to be:

A   a journalist

B   a hotel receptionist

C   a garden designer

D   a nurse

E   a chemist

F   a sales assistant

Speaker 1		19
Speaker 2		20
Speaker 3		21
Speaker 4		22
Speaker 5		23

PART 4

You will hear a conversation between a father, a mother and their son.
For questions 24–30, decide who expresses each idea and mark F for the father,
M for the mother and S for the son.

24 Who admires the action of some neighbours?

24

25 Who suggests the neighbours are foolish?

25

26 Who dislikes the place where they live?

26

27 Who has practical objections to moving?

27

28 Who explains someone else's idea?

28

29 Who hopes to be invited by the neighbours?

29

30 Who believes the neighbours are showing off?

30

PAPER 5 SPEAKING (14 minutes)

Part 1

You tell the examiner about yourself. The examiner may ask you questions such as: Where are you from? How do you usually spend your free time? What are your plans for the future? Your partner does the same.

Part 2

The examiner gives you two pictures to look at and asks you to talk about them for about a minute. Your partner does the same with two different pictures.

Part 3

The examiner gives you a photograph or drawing to look at with your partner. You are asked to solve a problem or come to a decision about something in the picture. For example, you might be asked to decide which of two rooms should be used as a study area and which as a leisure area. You discuss the problem together.

Part 4

You are asked more questions connected with your discussion in Part 3. For example, you may be asked to talk about the best ways of studying.

Practice Test 2

PAPER 1 READING (1 hour 15 minutes)

PART 1

*You are going to read a magazine article about a sportsman who is a champion hurdler. Choose the most suitable heading from the list (**A–I**) for each part (**1–7**) of the article. There is one extra heading which you do not need to use. There is an example at the beginning (**0**).*

*Mark your answers **on the separate answer sheet**.*

A	A regular practice routine
B	Concern about the future
C	Not enough time in the day
D	Doing better than ever
E	International living
F	The daily routine varies
G	Home and work
H	Impatience sometimes wins
I	What I eat

My kind of day

0	*I*

Sometimes I don't eat for a couple of days – it's a personal thing that's developed over the past few years. It seems to me that people often eat out of habit, not because they're hungry. I'll often have a low-fat yoghurt in the morning and sometimes turkey or pasta in the evening.

1	

Home is a four-bedroom detached house in Rhoose in the Vale of Glamorgan, near Cardiff, where I was born. I also have a condominium in Toronto, a flat in Richmond, Surrey, where my sister Suzanne lives, and a house in Florida, which is where I train in the winter. My friend Mark McKoy, the Olympic 110 metres hurdles champion, encouraged me to get a place in Toronto and I love it there. It's where I'd like to end my days.

2	

My father Ossie, a retired sales supervisor, and my mum Angela, a nurse, live with me in Rhoose but I have my own office where I work for Nuff Respect, the sports marketing and PR company that I run with my friend Linford

Christie. The name comes from a street expression that kids often say to us, meaning congratulations, our respect goes out to you.

3

I'm up about 8am and in training by 10am. Most days in the summer, I go to Cardiff Athletics Stadium with my hurdles partner Paul Gray. I usually drive into Cardiff in my Toyota Supra, pick up Paul and go to the track. We put the hurdles up – glamorous life, isn't it? – do an hour of stretching exercises and get into the hurdles work.

4

Hurdling is a natural thing – I think you have to be born with it. You need to combine a runner's speed with a dancer's grace. Getting technically more efficient is the only way to keep improving and I'm in excellent shape at the moment. I'm confident I can break my 110 metres hurdles world record this summer – in Zurich on 17 August, in Brussels two days later or at the Commonwealth Games on 22 August. There could even be three new world records in a week. Then I'll be focusing on the next Olympics.

5

In the afternoon I do some work for Nuff Respect, using my computer and fax machine. I enjoy the work – after all, I'm the product being marketed – but I have a severe problem with unprofessional people. Usually I'm quite relaxed, but I'll shout at those who waste my time.

6

When the work's finished, I'll shower, change, ask my father what he's doing and maybe pick up Mum from University Hospital. Later, I may drop into Paul's house and cook for him and his family. I cook whatever's there – it's the only artistic thing I do. But I rarely eat it myself.

7

Back home, I'll watch late-night television until I feel tired. I always go to sleep thinking about what the next day holds. Sometimes it seems like a circus, a fantasy world. All I can do is run fast – is that a real kind of world? It certainly won't last forever.

*You are going to read the beginning of a short story. For questions **8–14**, choose the answer (**A**, **B**, **C** or **D**) which you think fits best according to the text. Mark your answers **on the separate answer sheet**.*

ILIVED WITH Mother in a large white house surrounded by tall trees. It was a long walk to the nearest buildings as we were beyond the outskirts of town. It seems to me now that I would ask myself whether we needed to live as we did, she in this lonely white house leading her life, me elsewhere in that same large house, being me. Her child. I suppose in all those years I may have asked myself that, and yet I suspect, in reality, I scarcely gave it any thought.

One day, soon after my thirtieth birthday, Mother told me that she had sold the house. She had found somewhere else, she said. She did not mention where. I did not ask.

Shortly after, two very willing removal men arrived with an orange van which they promptly began loading up with furniture and boxes. Mother directed them from the house. I stood outside underneath our tall trees and watched, fascinated by the process. Many of the things which these strangers were steadily lifting up and taking away had never been moved before in all my lifetime. Indeed, until that moment, I don't think it ever occurred to me that these things could actually be moved. The house and everything in it had seemed so completely fixed. When I saw that the van was nearly full I went indoors to find Mother.

'Keep anything you like,' she said to me. 'I've taken all I want.'

'Thank you,' I said.

'The new people should be here tomorrow.' She climbed into the van alongside the two men, the engine started and they drove away.

Next day, as Mother said they would, a couple came. They were obviously a bit annoyed to find me there. I packed some necessities into a small brown leather suitcase that I did not know was still in the house until I found it. I felt them watch me as I walked away down the path and along the road that eventually led to the railway station.

It had been a long quiet walk so I was surprised when I found the station busy with activity. I had expected to sit for a while and calmly decide my next course of action but a quick glance round the station told me that queuing for a ticket was the first thing for all newcomers to do – buying a cup of tea and trying to find a seat on the platform the next. The queue was long and appeared to move forward only slowly. All well and good, I thought, taking my place behind a woman who was engaged in a fierce argument with her husband while trying to keep several children in order.

'Everyone!' he repeated sarcastically. The husband looked angrily around and as I stood up he caught my eye. I was now part of the argument against him.

'Yes, everyone – so you might just as well make up your mind to enjoy yourself, Harold.'

'I certainly will!' Harold spat back. 'And it won't be with you either!' he told his wife. It was all very public and rather shocking.

'Where to?' The family had reached the front of the queue.

'Two and three halves, returns to Southpool,' the woman declared. Harold was called upon to pay. This he did by counting out the money as slowly as it is possible to count out money. The queue heaved impatiently.

'Where to?'

'Southpool,' I said without a moment's hesitation.

'One way, or are you coming back?' he asked.

'One way,' I said. I was almost surprised when he handed me the ticket. When I had paid, I had half an hour to wait and enough

money for a cup of tea. During that half
90 hour, I reckoned it like this: All these people
going to the seaside would be eating teas in
little cafés along the sea front. Other people
would be employed to serve those teas.
The train was packed. I was lucky and
managed to squeeze myself on to a seat. I 95
did not see Harold and his family again.

8 When the author was a child, how did she feel about her mother's coldness?
  A She wished her mother were different.
  B She didn't let it bother her.
  C She tried to change their lives.
  D She wondered if she was really her mother.

9 What does 'it' in line 11 refer to?
  A the way she treated her mother
  B the town
  C the way they lived
  D the house

10 How did the author feel when she watched their things going into the van?
  A surprised at how easily their home was taken apart
  B worried about what was going to happen
  C glad her mother was going
  D concerned that the men should do their job properly

11 The author was still in the house when the new people came because she
  A didn't want to go with her mother.
  B hadn't arranged to leave until the day after her mother.
  C hadn't made any plans.
  D didn't want to leave the house.

12 Why did she buy a ticket as soon as she got to the station?
  A because there was nowhere to sit down
  B because she was in a hurry to catch her train
  C because that was what everyone else was doing
  D because she wanted to get away from the crowd

13 Why did she disapprove of the family?
  A because they did not have much money
  B because the children were badly behaved
  C because they did not speak to her
  D because they were arguing in front of other people

14 Why did she feel she had chosen the right place to go?
  A because she hadn't been to Southpool before
  B because she thought she could get a job in Southpool
  C because she was looking forward to having tea by the sea
  D because she couldn't afford to go further

PART 3

You are going to read a magazine article about sand. Eight sentences have been removed from the article. Choose from the sentences (**A–I**) the one which fits each gap (**15–21**). There is one extra sentence which you do not need to use. There is an example at the beginning (**0**).

Mark your answers **on the separate answer sheet**.

Sands of time

Sand: as children we play on it and as adults we relax on it. It is something we complain about when it gets in our eyes on a windy beach, and praise when it is made into sand castles. **0** | *I* | If we did, we would discover an account of a geological past and a history of sea life that goes back thousands and, in some cases, millions of years.

Sand covers not just seashores, but also ocean beds, deserts and mountains. **15** | | And it is a major element in manufactured products too – concrete is largely sand, while glass is made of little else. **16** | | Well, it is larger than fine dust and smaller than shingle. In fact, according to the most generally accepted scheme of measurement, grains can be called sand if their diameter is greater than 0.06 of a millimetre and less than 0.6 of a millimetre.

Depending on its age and origin, a particular sand can consist of tiny stones or porous grains through which water can pass. **17** | | They have come from the breaking down of rocks, or from the dead bodies of sea creatures, which collect on the bottom of the oceans, or even from volcanic eruptions.

18 | | If it is a dazzling white, its grains may come from nearby coral, from crystalline quartz rocks or from gypsum, like the white sand of New Mexico. On Pacific Islands, jet black sands form from volcanic minerals. Other black beaches are magnetic and are mined for iron ore.

19 [   ] It washes rock into streams and rivers and down to the sea, leaving behind softer materials. By the time it reaches the sea, the hardest rocks remain but everything else has been broken into tiny particles of 0.02 millimetre diameter or less. The largest pieces fall to the bottom quickly, while smaller particles float and settle only slowly in deeper water, which is why the sandy beach on the shoreline so often turns to mud further out.

20 [   ] If the individual fragments still have sharp edges, you can be sure they were formed fairly recently. This is the case on the island of Kamoama in Hawaii, where a beach was created after a volcanic eruption in 1990. Molten lava spilled into the sea and exploded into glassy droplets.

It seems that when the poet William Blake saw infinity in a grain of sand he was not far wrong. Sand is an irreplaceable industrial ingredient which has many uses. **21** [   ] Sand cushions our land from the force of the sea, and geologists say it often does a better job protecting our shores than the most advanced coastal technology.

A These may have the shape of stars or spirals, their edges rough or smooth.

B It is one of the most common substances on earth.

C In addition, it has one vital function which you might never even notice.

D Rain is an important force in the creation of beaches.

E In the great slow cycle of the earth, sand that was once rock can turn to rock again.

F What exactly is sand?

G Colour is another clue to the origins of sand.

H It can be difficult to date the sand on a beach accurately but it is possible to get a general idea of whether or not the sand is 'young' or 'old'.

I But we don't often look at it.

PART 4

*You are going to read a magazine article about television programmes. For questions **22–35**, choose from the programmes (**A–F**). There is an example at the beginning (**0**).*
*Mark your answers **on the separate answer sheet**.*

Which programme:

gives you recipes from different parts of the world every week?	**0**	*A*
is set in different places?	**22**	
is aimed at beginners?	**23**	
may soon be shown more frequently?	**24**	
involves the presenter's family?	**25**	
tells you about things that can go wrong?	**26**	
contains nothing about cookery?	**27**	
gives information about food production?	**28**	
advises on healthy eating?	**29**	
regularly invites another professional to appear with the presenter?	**30**	
will not continue after its present series?	**31**	
has been critical of some cookery experts?	**32**	
cannot be seen in every television area at the moment?	**33**	
looks at different ways of using one particular food?	**34**	
is very thorough in its research?	**35**	

March's food, health and fitness on the box

A   FOOD FILE

Food File tells you exactly what goes into the food on your plate, as the programme follows it from farmyard to factory and finally to your front door. Nutritionist Amanda Ursell returns on Wednesday to present a third series of the popular programme that leaves no lid unlifted and no dishcloth unturned. Last time she told us about the killer bug that lives in hamburgers, asked why we don't always get a good deal from restaurants, complained about cookery writers whose recipes don't work and told us about a new approach to dieting. Plus, there are recipes from around the world as a regular feature.

B   YOU CAN COOK

Who can bone a chicken in 30 seconds or less, create a Chinese banquet before your eyes and tell you all there is to know about Asian cuisine? Yan can! Chinese-American chef Martin Yan – cookery teacher, cookbook author and host of the hit ITV afternoon series *You Can Cook* – has been seen on nearly all the ITV regions in recent years. Just lately he's been seen once a week in the Anglia and Central regions. If he isn't on your screen right now, he soon will be again. Martin is seen preparing dishes with an Oriental touch, assisted each week by a different guest such as San Francisco Thai cooking expert Joyce Jue or sausage expert Bruce Aidells. Even his mother and his uncle get in on the act.

C   HEALTHWATCH

Latest ideas on the health front are the subject of this new monthly programme which began in December as part of Sky News and is now likely to go fortnightly. The series kicked off with reports on noise pollution, doctors who leave Britain, eye surgery, hospital waiting lists and predicting heart attacks by computer. Presenter Nicola Hill recently introduced another welcome idea from the medical hotline – doctors who prescribe exercises instead of drugs.

D   A TASTE OF AFRICA

Presenter Dorinda Hafner cooks nesting pigeons – a favourite recipe from her childhood – when she visits Egypt for her Channel 4 series. Continuing on Wednesdays until March 23, the programme takes viewers to Tanzania for a four-course meal featuring bananas in every course, plus banana wine to wash it down, and to Zanzibar where visitors can try a lipstick straight from the lipstick tree. In Mali, Dorinda visits the River Niger to see the hippo, the country's national symbol, and cook a fine freshwater fish, the capitaine. And there's another series to come later in the year.

E   SIMPLY DELICIOUS

Chef Darina Allen has been running her half-hour cookery programmes every weekday at 9 am throughout February on The Learning Channel, covering dishes for family and friends, fish meals and French and Italian food. The final series continues until March 4 with specialities like *bœuf bourguignon* from France and *tiramisu* from Italy, with instructions for people who have never cooked a thing in their lives.

F   FOOD AND DRINK

Chefs, wine tasters and other specialists gather together for another round-up of recipes, food news, drinks tips and product tastings. Water prices, wine in pubs, the dangers of dieting and ways of eating to prevent heart disease and minimise the effects of smoking are some of the topics covered so far in this series.

PAPER 2   WRITING (1 hour 30 minutes)

PART 1

*You **must** answer this question.*

1   You and your friends have just finished a course and you want to arrange a party. You've had a meeting and made a list of your requirements. You've heard that your friends, Anna and Jack, who attend a nearby school, had a party on a boat last term and you want to ask them all about it.

Read your notes carefully. Then write to Anna and Jack telling them what you want to do and asking for information and advice.

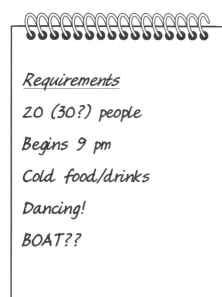

Requirements

20 (30?) people

Begins 9 pm

Cold food/drinks

Dancing!

BOAT??

Ask Anna and Jack
Numbers?
Transport to river?
Food?
Music?
How much? Worth it?
Their opinions?

Write a **letter** of between **120–180** words in an appropriate style on the next page. Do not write any addresses.

PART 1

PART 2

Write an answer to **one** *of the questions* **2–5** *in this part. Write your answer in* **120–180** *words in an appropriate style on the next page, putting the question number in the box.*

2   A student magazine is running a series entitled **Books I have loved**, which includes reviews of favourite books by its readers.

Write a **review** of one of your favourite books, explaining what you like about it.

3   Your class has been discussing the importance of possessions. For homework, your teacher has asked you to write a composition, describing two of your favourite possessions and explaining what each of them means to you.

Write your **composition**.

4

> # Radio LGC ═══════
>
> *We would like to receive short reports from listeners for a future series of programmes on travel experiences called* **My most exciting journey**.
>
> *Reports must include practical details about the journey and describe any interesting incidents which happened on the way.*

Write your **report** for the radio programme.

5   **Background reading texts**

Answer **one** of the following two questions based on your reading of **one** of the set books (see p. v). Write the title of the book next to the question number box.

Either   **(a)** How important to the story is the period in which it is set?

or   **(b)** Describe a character in the book whom you dislike, and explain why.

PART 2

Question	

....

....

....

....

....

....

....

....

....

....

....

....

....

....

....

....

....

....

....

....

....

....

....

....

....

....

PAPER 3   USE OF ENGLISH (1 hour 15 minutes)

PART 1

For questions **1–15**, *read the text below and decide which answer* **A, B, C** *or* **D**
best fits each space. There is an example at the beginning (**0**).
Mark your answers **on the separate answer sheet**.

Example:

0   **A** in   **B** of   **C** with   **D** for

0	A	B	C	D
	▬	▭	▭	▭

AN AUSTRALIAN MYSTERY

Interest **(0)** …. undiscovered human-like creatures continues to be widespread.
Everyone has **(1)** …. of the Yeti, and its North American 'cousin' Bigfoot, but since the
last century there have been **(2)** …. of the existence in Australia of another, less
famous creature – the Yahoo. In 1912, a Sydney newspaper **(3)** …. an account by
Charles Harper of a strange, large animal he observed **(4)** …. the light of his campfire:
'Its body, legs, and arms were covered with long, brownish-red hair, but what **(5)** ….
me as most extraordinary was its shape, which was human in some ways, **(6)** …. at
the same time very different. The body was enormous, **(7)** …. great strength. The
arms were extremely long and very muscular.'

Harper continued: 'All this observation **(8)** …. a few minutes while the creature stood
there, as if frightened by the firelight. After a few growls, and beating his breast, he
(9) …. , the first few metres upright, then on all four limbs through the low bushes.
Nothing **(10)** …. persuade my companions **(11)** …. the trip, a fact at which I must
admit I was rather pleased.'

What could Harper and his companions **(12)** …. have seen? Such a creature was
(13) …. in south-eastern Australia in the 1800s, but no specimen was ever obtained
for scientific **(14)** …. , and all we are **(15)** …. with today is an historical puzzle.

1 **A** understood **B** known **C** heard **D** noticed

2 **A** statements **B** reports **C** arguments **D** proofs

3 **A** delivered **B** typed **C** declared **D** printed

4 **A** by **B** at **C** with **D** under

5 **A** marked **B** struck **C** touched **D** knocked

6 **A** even **B** just **C** still **D** yet

7 **A** announcing **B** pointing **C** indicating **D** describing

8 **A** lasted **B** covered **C** involved **D** engaged

9 **A** set back **B** set up **C** set in **D** set off

10 **A** should **B** must **C** might **D** would

11 **A** continue **B** to continue **C** continuing **D** having continued

12 **A** probably **B** likely **C** possibly **D** doubtless

13 **A** referred **B** mentioned **C** related **D** remarked

14 **A** arrangements **B** designs **C** plans **D** purposes

15 **A** left **B** found **C** seen **D** met

PART 2

*For questions **16–30**, read the text below and think of the word which best fits each space. Use only **one** word in each space. There is an example at the beginning (**0**).*
*Write your word **on the separate answer sheet**.*

Example:

0	*it*	0

FAMILY PHOTOGRAPHS

A family portrait is a valuable picture – **(0)** …. is fun to look at now, it's great for relatives far **(16)** …. , and it will bring back memories in the years to come. Families change quickly as children grow, **(17)** …. don't wait, whatever your position in the family – photograph your family group now, and plan to make this **(18)** …. regular event. Your family album isn't really complete **(19)** …. this record of all of you together.

Getting the **(20)** …. of the family together isn't always easy, and so you will need to plan ahead to be sure **(21)** …. has time to pose. A relaxed, friendly feeling is **(22)** …. makes the picture, and you can't expect people to relax **(23)** …. they're in a hurry to do **(24)** …. else. Make your plans when you're all together and **(25)** …. a cheerful, friendly mood – say, during a meal, and set a time convenient **(26)** …. everyone.

A family portrait takes some technical planning, too. Make **(27)** …. your mind in advance **(28)** …. room you want to use; choose your camera position and check the lighting. If you want to be in the picture, make sure you know exactly **(29)** …. the self-timer on your camera operates. With most cameras, you'll have from eight **(30)** …. twelve seconds to get into the picture after you press the shutter button.

PART 3

For questions **31–40***, complete the second sentence so that it has a similar meaning to the first sentence, using the word given.* **Do not change the word given***. You must use between two and five words, including the word given. There is an example at the beginning (***0***).*
Write **only** *the missing words* **on the separate answer sheet***.*

Example:

0   The tennis star ignored her coach's advice.
    attention

    The tennis star didn't .... her coach's advice.

The gap can be filled by the words 'pay any attention to' so you write:

0	*pay any attention to*	0	0 1 2

---

31   It would be difficult for me to finish the work by the weekend.
    difficulty

    I .... the work by the weekend.

32   Harry's home is still in Spain, is it?
    lives

    Harry .... he?

33   When Sandra walked out of the meeting, she didn't say goodbye to anyone.
    without

    Sandra left .... goodbye to anyone.

34   You can borrow my bike if you're in a hurry.
    mind

    I .... you my bike if you're in a hurry.

35   Angus rarely takes a holiday.
    rare

    It .... take a holiday.

36 We lost the game because of my mistake.
fault

It was .... win the game.

37 Are you planning to do anything on Saturday?
plans

Do .... Saturday?

38 Tim looks nothing like his father.
take

Tim .... his father at all.

39 The film I saw last week was better than this one.
good

This film .... the one I saw last week.

40 I regret giving Dennis my phone number.
Dennis

I wish .... my phone number.

PART 4

*For questions **41–55**, read the text below and look carefully at each line. Some of the lines are correct, and some have a word which should not be there. If a line is correct, put a tick (✓) by the number **on the separate answer sheet**. If a line has a word which should **not** be there, write the word **on the separate answer sheet**. There are two examples at the beginning (**0** and **00**).*

Examples:

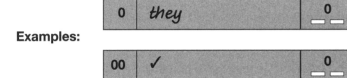

THE TROUBLE WITH GOING TO THE CINEMA

0	I don't like the cinema very much myself, but my friends they all
00	love it, and so I often find myself sitting in the dark trying to follow
41	through the conversation on the screen while sweet papers and
42	crisp packets are being opened enthusiastically all around me.
43	It is this sort of annoying disturbance at the cinema which it means
44	that I'd rather prefer to hire a video and watch it at home. Then there
45	is no risk of getting cross because it's impossible to hear anything
46	what is going on. Another problem is that I always do my own best to
47	find a seat with a good view of the screen during the advertisements.
48	Then, at two minutes before the main film is due to begin, the seat in
49	front of me will be taken by a heavyweight boxer who blocks out
50	most of the screen and so, by this time, it's too late to move. I know
51	how this isn't really the point. Cinema fans talk about the extra
52	pleasure of an experience is shared with others. I must admit
53	because there's often a very good atmosphere in the cinema, and
54	I'm probably too sensitive to these things: it only takes up one
55	person making stupid comments to spoil me the whole occasion. On
	balance, I think I'll stick to my video!

For questions **56–65**, read the text below. Use the word given in capitals at the end of each line to form a word that fits in the space in the same line. There is an example at the beginning (**0**). Write your word **on the separate answer sheet**.

Example:

0	*imperfect*	0

JOB INTERVIEWS

Interviews are an **(0)** .... method of choosing the best people for jobs,   **PERFECT**
yet human **(56)** .... like to examine each other in this way. One of the   **BE**
many problems of **(57)** .... as it is commonly practised is that the forms   **SELECT**
filled in by **(58)** .... often fail to show people as they really are. This   **APPLY**
means that you can follow all the best **(59)** .... when completing your   **ADVISE**
form and still find that you are **(60)** .... at the next stage – the interview.   **SUCCESS**
(61) .... , in the rare cases where interviews are automatic, a candidate   **SIMILAR**
with an **(62)** .... form may do surprisingly well.   **ADEQUATE**

Of course, your form needs to show that you have **(63)** .... in your   **CONFIDENT**
(64) .... to do the job, but don't try to turn yourself into someone else – a   **ABLE**
person you have to pretend to be at the interview. Realism and **(65)** .... are   **HONEST**
definitely the best approach.

PAPER 4   LISTENING (approximately 40 minutes)

PART 1

You'll hear people talking in eight different situations.
*For questions **1–8**, choose the best answer **A**, **B** or **C**.*

1   This woman is talking on the telephone.
Who is she speaking to?

   A   her landlord

   B   an architect

   C   a builder

                1

2   On holiday, you hear another tourist describing a journey.
How did he feel?

   A   shocked

   B   embarrassed

   C   scared

                 2

3   You hear these people talking in a café.
Why did the man change his newspaper?

   A   the cost

   B   the opinions

   C   the quality of the writing

                 3

4   This woman is phoning a friend about the date of a meeting.
Why has she called?

   A   to apologise for changing it

   B   to inform her about changing it

   C   to explain the reason for changing it

                 4

5 You hear a girl talking about clothes.
What is she describing?

    A a coat

    B a dress

    C a trouser suit

        5

6 Listen to this film critic.
What does he like least about the film?

    A the characters

    B the action scenes

    C the main story

        6

7 You hear these people talking while queuing in a shop.
What does the woman complain about?

    A the payment system

    B the service

    C the quality of the goods

        7

8 You hear these people talking about a book.
Who is the book about?

    A a poet

    B a song writer

    C a journalist

        8

PART 2

You will hear two students who want to be chosen as student representative in their college.
*For questions **9–18**, complete the notes. You will need to write a word or a short phrase.*

Linda wants the college
to offer better advice on | **9**

Students need more
information about jobs | **10**

She thinks students don't
have enough chances to | **11**

She'd like students to
raise money for people who | **12**

She wants to
improve the facilities in the | **13**

Darren intends to
prevent a rise in the price of | **14**

He wants to set up | **15**

He thinks the college lacks | **16**

He criticises the
way the college handles | **17**

He'd like to
invite a greater variety of | **18**

PART 3

You will hear five people talking about sport.
*For questions **19–23**, choose from the list **A–F** what they say. Use the letters only once. There is one extra letter which you do not need to use.*

This speaker:

A   has taken up sport as a way of meeting people

B   watches sport in order to relax

Speaker 1	19
Speaker 2	20
Speaker 3	21
Speaker 4	22
Speaker 5	23

C   organises sport for his or her friends

D   organises sport as part of a job

E   does sport in order to keep fit

F   watches sport with friends

PART 4

You will hear a local radio report about places to eat.
For questions 24–30, choose the best answer A, B or C.

24 When should you order a picnic pack from Ali?

    A by lunchtime
    B the day before
    C early in the morning

    24

25 What does Caroline criticise about 'Chick'n'things'?

    A the quality of the food
    B the value for money
    C the speed of service

    25

26 At 'Pat's Café' you are most likely to meet

    A lorry drivers.
    B people on walking tours.
    C commuters.

    26

27 Why couldn't Caroline continue her research after her breakfast?

    A She was ill.
    B She wasn't hungry.
    C She had a long drive home.

    27

28 What did Caroline enjoy at the 'Old Mill'?

    A the coffee
    B the cakes
    C the view

    28

29 What does she mention about the 'Food Box'?

    A She eats there quite often.
    B She's a friend of the owner.
    C She likes to go there on special occasions.

    29

30 What is the problem for customers of the 'Four Seasons'?

    A Parking is difficult.
    B The neighbourhood is rather rough.
    C The staff don't seem to care about the customers.

    30

PAPER 5   SPEAKING (14 minutes)

Part 1

You tell the examiner about yourself. The examiner may ask you questions such as: Where are you from? How do you usually spend your free time? What are your plans for the future? Your partner does the same.

Part 2

The examiner gives you two pictures to look at and asks you to talk about them for about a minute. Your partner does the same with two different pictures.

Part 3

The examiner gives you a photograph or drawing to look at with your partner. You are asked to solve a problem or come to a decision about something in the picture. For example, you might be asked to decide which of two rooms should be used as a study area and which as a leisure area. You discuss the problem together.

Part 4

You are asked more questions connected with your discussion in Part 3. For example, you may be asked to talk about the best ways of studying.

Practice Test 3

PAPER 1   READING (1 hour 15 minutes)

PART 1

*You are going to read an article from a consumer magazine about the London underground railway. Choose the most suitable heading from the list (**A–H**) for each part (**1–6**) of the article. There is one extra heading which you do not need to use. There is an example at the beginning (**0**).*
*Mark your answers **on the separate answer sheet**.*

A	Poor announcements
B	Dirty and outdated
C	Passengers' opinions count
D	Occasional users
E	Overcrowded
F	A waste of time
G	Unreliable
H	Under pressure

THE SERVICE YOU GET ON THE TUBE

0	*H*

THE WORLD'S first underground railway (the Tube) opened in London in January 1863. Today there are 11 lines serving 272 stations, the busiest of which, King's Cross, sees the start and finish of around 70 million journeys a year. But the system is in crisis – mainly as a result of underinvestment. Overcrowding combined with poor reliability can lead to problems for travellers, particularly those who use the Tube during its busiest hours.

1	

This report looks at service and safety on the Underground. It's based on the findings of our survey of passengers. Last June we interviewed 1,698 Tube travellers outside 46 Underground stations in London; 517 regular travellers (those using the Tube throughout the year on three or more days each week) were contacted again and asked more detailed questions by phone.

2	

Since 1981 the number of passengers using the Tube has increased by almost half. The increase in passengers has not been matched by an expansion of the Underground system and there is widespread congestion, particularly during the six peak hours when over 60 per cent of all journeys are made. London Underground Limited (LU) states that over the busiest rush hour no more than one person should have to stand for each seated passenger. But LU's own statistics show that this standard is often not met over large areas of track on a daily basis.

Forty-three per cent of regular travellers had missed an appointment or been late for something in the two weeks before the survey because of delays on the Underground.

Forty-three per cent of regular travellers mentioned graffiti, rubbish and generally dirty conditions as one of the aspects of the Underground's service they disliked. The aim set by Government for train cleaning is that carriages should be cleaned internally every day they are in use. LU's figures show it has come very close to achieving this. But there are no standards to define or measure how well trains have been cleaned. LU has made progress in dealing with rubbish at major stations but graffiti, old coaches and unmodernised stations remain serious problems.

Well over half of the regular travellers said they were dissatisfied with the information provided when something goes wrong on the system; 72 per cent of those who were dissatisfied complained that the information was wrong or given too late; 49 per cent couldn't hear or understand what was said. LU told us that a new system has been installed, which should mean clearer messages. However, the new system applies only to messages broadcast within stations; those coming from a central control room may not improve for some time to come.

Most of this report reflects the experiences of regular Tube travellers but we also asked those who do not travel every day for their views. The most popular type of ticket bought by these travellers was a one-day pass. Few appeared to have had problems finding their way around the system – 89 per cent said finding their way around was 'easy'.

PART 2

*You are going to read an article about a photographer. For questions **7–14**, choose the answer (**A**, **B**, **C** or **D**) which you think fits best according to the text. Mark your answers **on the separate answer sheet**.*

Biologically Correct

MY LOVE OF NATURE goes right back to my childhood, to the times when I stayed on my grandparents' farm in Suffolk. My father was in the armed forces, so we were always moving and didn't have a home base for any length of time, but I loved going there. I think it was my grandmother who encouraged me more than anyone: she taught me the names of wildflowers and got me interested in looking at the countryside, so it seemed obvious to go on to do Zoology at university.

I didn't get my first camera until after I'd graduated, when I was due to go diving in Norway and needed a method of recording the sea creatures I would find there. My father didn't know anything about photography, but he bought me an Exacta, which was really quite a good camera for the time, and I went off to take my first pictures of sea anemones and starfish. I became keen very quickly, and learned how to develop and print; obviously I didn't have much money in those days, so I did more black-and-white photography than colour, but it was all still using the camera very much as a tool to record what I found both by diving and on the shore. I had no ambition at all to be a photographer then, or even for some years afterwards.

Unlike many of the wildlife photographers of the time, I trained as a scientist and therefore my way of expressing myself is very different. I've tried from the beginning

35 to produce pictures which are always biologically correct. There are people who will alter things deliberately: you don't pick up sea creatures from the middle of the shore and take them down to attractive
40 pools at the bottom of the shore without knowing you're doing it. In so doing you're actually falsifying the sort of seaweeds they live on and so on, which may seem unimportant but it is actually changing the
45 natural surroundings to make them prettier. Unfortunately, many of the people who select pictures are looking for attractive images and, at the end of the day, whether it's truthful or not doesn't really matter to
50 them.

It's important to think about the animal first, and there are many occasions when I've not taken a picture because it would have been too disturbing. Nothing is so important
55 that you have to get that shot; of course, there are cases when it would be very sad if you didn't, but it's not the end of the world. There can be a lot of ignorance in people's behaviour towards wild animals and it's a
60 problem that more and more people are going to wild places: while some animals may get used to cars, they won't get used to people suddenly rushing up to them. The sheer pressure of people, coupled with the fact that there are increasingly few places 65 where no-one else has photographed, means that over the years, life has become much more difficult for the professional wildlife photographer.

Nevertheless, wildlife photographs play a 70 very important part in educating people about what is out there and what needs conserving. Although photography can be an enjoyable pastime, as it is to many people, it is also something that plays a very 75 important part in educating young and old alike. Of the qualities it takes to make a good wildlife photographer, patience is perhaps the most obvious – you just have to be prepared to sit it out. I'm actually more 80 patient now because I write more than ever before, and as long as I've got a bit of paper and a pencil, I don't feel I'm wasting my time. And because I photograph such a wide range of things, even if the main target 85 doesn't appear I can probably find something else to concentrate on instead.

7 Heather Angel decided to go to university and study Zoology because
  A she wanted to improve her life in the countryside.
  B she was persuaded to do so by her grandmother.
  C she was keen on the natural world.
  D she wanted to stop moving around all the time.

8 Why did she get her first camera?
  A She needed to be able to look back at what she had seen.
  B She wanted to find out if she enjoyed photography.
  C Her father thought it was a good idea for her to have one.
  D She wanted to learn how to use one and develop her own prints.

9 How is she different from some of the other wildlife photographers she meets?
  A She tries to make her photographs as attractive as possible.
  B She takes photographs which record accurate natural conditions.
  C She likes to photograph plants as well as wildlife.
  D She knows the best places to find wildlife.

10 What does 'them' refer to in line 45?

    A sea creatures

    B attractive pools

    C seaweeds

    D natural surroundings

11 Heather Angel now finds it more difficult to photograph wild animals because

    A there are fewer of them.

    B they have become more nervous of people.

    C it is harder to find suitable places.

    D they have become frightened of cars.

12 Wildlife photography is important because it can make people realise that

    A photography is an enjoyable hobby.

    B we learn little about wildlife at school.

    C it is worthwhile visiting the countryside.

    D it is important to look after wild animals.

13 Why is she more patient now?

    A She does other things while waiting.

    B She has got used to waiting.

    C She can concentrate better than she used to.

    D She knows the result will be worth it.

14 Which of the following describes Heather Angel?

    A proud

    B sensitive

    C aggressive

    D disappointed

PART 3

*You are going to read a newspaper article about a family who live on a farm. Seven paragraphs have been removed from the article. Choose from the paragraphs (**A–H**) the one which fits each gap (**15–20**). There is one extra paragraph which you do not need to use. There is an example at the beginning (**0**). Mark your answers **on the separate answer sheet**.*

Ice-cream that keeps the family together

It is a bitter November evening and the westerly winds are howling across south-west England from the Atlantic Ocean. In the warmth of their old stone farmhouse the Roskilly family's thoughts are turned to summer.

0	*H*

'It's a bit unusual but it's worth a try next summer,' says Rachel Roskilly, 59. No-one disagrees with her. Next summer the new flavour of ice-cream will be added to the 33 flavours of ice-cream that the family already produces.

15	

The herd of cows that is the base of the family

business is his main activity. There are 90 prime milkers, and 60 calves complete the herd.

16	

Soon after, in 1960, Joe married Rachel. He has added 45 hectares to the farm but has not gone far from his home. 'This year I have not been out of Cornwall,' he said. 'Rachel and I last had a holiday when our son Toby was four. There has just been too much to do.'

17	

'Although we had been making clotted cream since we married and doing holiday lets in the outbuildings for 32 years, we realised that if the farm was ever to support three grown-up children plus their possible families we had to make it a lot more profitable,' Joe said.

18	

'We had decided against ice-cream in 1984 because small-scale equipment was not available at the right price,' Joe said. 'But three years later, when we were looking for a small pasteurising machine with which to make whipping cream, we realised that things had changed.'

19	

In addition, last summer the family opened The

Croust House, a 50-seater restaurant serving coffee, cream teas, salads and other light lunches, as well as all the ice-creams and Rachel's home-made bread, scones, cakes and jams.

20	

'Although the cows are the key to everything we do, I have always felt that being ready to change and expand when necessary makes farming more interesting and more fun than it used to be. The younger generation can get bored by the routine of farming. We can keep their interest by bringing in new ideas when otherwise they might have been tempted away from the countryside.'

A Hard work and money have not always gone hand in hand at Tregellast Barton farm. Ten years ago Rachel and Joe were making a turnover of under £50,000 – less than a fifth of what they turn over now.

B Two years ago Bryn, who had gained a degree at the Royal College of Art, was tempted back to the farm by the offer of her own stained glass studio. Toby returned this year from a furniture making course to set up a furniture workshop.

C 'It is very labour-intensive and it is too early to say how it is doing financially,' Joe said. 'But changing the use of some of the cow sheds cost us very little as we did most of the work ourselves.'

D He has been producing milk on the farm, 10 miles from Britain's most southerly point, since he came there to work for his godmother at 17. When she retired she gave Joe the farm of 20 hectares.

E 'Rachel and I invested £5,000 in a pasteurising machine and a deep freeze, convinced that making ice-cream would help keep the children's interest in the farm. It's been very successful.'

F Joe Roskilly, 63-year-old father of the family, sits at the end of the table in his farmer's overalls. He is silent, but under his shock of grey hair he is attentive.

G They looked at ways of making more money from their milk, and also from their Jersey cream, which had a good local reputation. Ice-cream seemed the best idea.

H Halva – the Middle Eastern sweet – is the subject of the conversation. Would it make a good ice-cream flavour? Rachel Roskilly thinks it would. Together with sons Jacob, 31, Toby, 25, and daughter Bryn, 29, she had been experimenting with halva, honey, nuts and their own milk and cream for much of the day.

PART 4

*You are going to read a magazine article about different types of guidebooks. For questions **21–35**, choose from the books (**A–G**). Some of the books may be chosen more than once. When more than one answer is required, these may be given in any order. There is an example at the beginning (**0**).*
*Mark your answers **on the separate answer sheet**.*

A	Blue Guides
B	Everyman Guides
C	Companion Guides
D	Cadogan Guides
E	Rough Guides
F	Lonely Planet series
G	Time Out series

Which type of guidebook:

is not modern in its approach?   **0** *C*

is attractive to look at?   **21**

offers unconventional views on famous buildings?   **22**

is not suitable for reading in advance?   **23**

does not help you find your way around a city?   **24**

has a style which might annoy some readers?   **25**

does not give complete coverage of the sights?   **26** **27**

takes you on a guided tour of the buildings it describes?   **28**

gives you a personal viewpoint?

29	

does not contain what you might at first expect?

30	

tells you the history of each building?

31	

contains examples of artists' work?

32	

is part of an expanding series?

33			34	

concentrates on entertainment?

35	

GUIDE to the GUIDES

A guidebook can make or break your holiday. The best will encourage, surprise and delight you, the worst can frustrate and annoy, leaving you lost and bored.

The **Blue Guides** are among the best-known cultural guides. They take you through museums room by room. Their tiny print goes into huge detail to describe the background of monuments that other guides ignore. This is really dull stuff. Curl up in bed with a Blue Guide and deep sleep is guaranteed within two pages. On holiday, however – as you stand curious before a small chapel in a backstreet of Rome – it is the only place to find out everything.

The new **Everyman Guides** cannot compete on detail, but they are a lot more fun. A riot of colour springs from the photographs, illustrations, maps and paintings accompanying the text. Visually they are amazing. In particular the Everyman city guides – such as Prague and Vienna – manage to catch the splendour of their subjects.

Both these series are highly functional, but they lack any real character. Not so the lovingly written, academic and very old-fashioned **Companion Guides**. A day in their company is rather like one spent with your (or at least my) favourite, rather mischievous aunt. Seriousness is always mixed with unexpected and pleasant surprises.

I particularly like the **Cadogan** series, rapidly growing now to cover almost all of Europe. Each one is written by an individual, not a team, which produces generally agreeable personal touches. They will take you down a Parisian side-street to tell you all about a particularly horrible 17th-century murderer or to point out a favourite cake shop. They are all about local colour and most readers will not mind their rushing of museums and missing altogether of lesser monuments.

Rough Guides offer the most successful practical coverage. Their recommendations can rarely be faulted and, as more books come out, their coverage of places of interest gets better. Rough Guides are written in a lively, jolly style about which traditionalists may complain. Prague Cathedral's tomb of St John, described in the Blue Guide as having 'unquestionably the finest furnishings of the time' and thought worthy of a full-page description, is described briefly in the Rough Guide as being a 'work of excess'. I prefer them to their main competitor, the **Lonely Planet** series, which does not even notice the tomb of St John.

The general guides mentioned so far are all arranged in a logical fashion that takes you clearly from place to place. The odd one out is the **Time Out** series. These guides are based on listings: restaurants one after another, shops, museums, nightclubs and so on. For the young, and the young at heart, they are invaluable.

PAPER 2 WRITING (1 hour 30 minutes)

PART 1

*You **must** answer this question.*

1   You have booked a holiday with a travel company, as advertised below, and have already paid in full. Two weeks before you are due to travel, you receive a letter from the company, informing you of changes to the holiday you have bought.

Read the advertisement below, together with the letter from the travel company. Then write to the travel company expressing your displeasure, and explaining why you expect to be given your money back.

Carefree
Holidays

Relax in the sunshine at the

Ocean Hotel

☆ Brand new luxury buildings

☆ Olympic-size swimming pool

☆ World-famous chef

☆ Dancing to big-name bands

Dear Sir/Madam,

We regret to inform you that, owing to circumstances beyond our control, building work at the Ocean Hotel will not be completed in time for your holiday. Sports and entertainment facilities will only be available in the second week, and then on a limited basis. Meals will be provided at a nearby restaurant.

We apologise for these changes, but feel sure that you will still have a wonderful time on your Carefree Holiday!

With best wishes

Brian McConnell

Brian McConnell
Carefree Holidays

Write a **letter** of between **120–180** words in an appropriate style on the next page. Do not write any addresses.

PART 1

PART 2

*Write an answer to **one** of the questions **2–5** in this part. Write your answer in*
***120–180** words in an appropriate style on the next page, putting the question*
number in the box.

2   As part of a project on family life, your teacher has asked you to write about a
    member of your family who has had a big influence on you.

    Describe the person and explain how their actions and character have been
    important to you.

3   Your local newspaper invites readers to send in short stories about their
    everyday experiences. The title they have chosen this week is: **Lost and
    found**.

    Write your **story** for the newspaper.

4   This is part of a letter you receive from a British friend who is studying your
    language in your country.

    > The course is great, but it's a bit formal. Do you have any advice
    > about how to improve my understanding of everyday language? I'd be
    > grateful for any suggestions.

    Write your **letter**, giving details of any newspapers, books, TV programmes,
    activities etc. you think might be useful and explaining how you would use
    them. Do not write any addresses.

5   **Background reading texts**

    Answer **one** of the following two questions based on your reading of **one** of
    the set books (see p. v). Write the title of the book next to the question
    number box.

    Either   **(a)** Describe the end of the story and say whether you expected the
                        book to finish in that way.

    or   **(b)** Which scene from the book would you choose to put on the
                        cover? Give your reasons.

PART 2

Question	

....
....
....
....
....
....
....
....
....
....
....
....
....
....
....
....
....
....
....
....
....
....
....
....
....
....
....
....
....

PAPER 3   USE OF ENGLISH (1 hour 15 minutes)

PART 1

*For questions **1–15**, read the text below and decide which answer **A, B, C** or **D**
best fits each space. There is an example at the beginning (**0**).
Mark your answers **on the separate answer sheet**.*

Example:

| 0 | **A** ever | **B** then | **C** also | **D** yet |

| 0 | A — | B — | C — | D — |

LOOK ON THE BRIGHT SIDE

Do you **(0)** .... wish you were more optimistic, someone who always **(1)** .... to be
successful? Having someone around who always **(2)** .... the worst isn't really a lot
of **(3)** .... – we all know someone who sees a single cloud on a sunny day and says,
'It looks **(4)** .... rain.' But if you catch yourself thinking such things, it's important to
do something **(5)** .... it.

You *can* change your view of life, **(6)** .... to psychologists. It only takes a little effort,
and you'll find life more rewarding as a **(7)** .... . Optimism, they say, is partly about
self-respect and confidence but it's also a more positive way of looking at life and
all it has to **(8)** .... . Optimists are more **(9)** .... to start new projects and are
generally more prepared to take risks.

Upbringing is obviously very important in forming your **(10)** .... to the world. Some
people are brought up to **(11)** .... too much on others and grow up forever blaming
other people when anything **(12)** .... wrong. Most optimists, on the **(13)** .... hand,
have been brought up not to **(14)** .... failure as the end of the world – they just
(15) .... with their lives.

1   **A** counted   **B** expected   **C** felt   **D** waited

2   **A** worries   **B** cares   **C** fears   **D** doubts

3   **A** amusement   **B** play   **C** enjoyment   **D** fun

4   **A** so   **B** to   **C** for   **D** like

5   **A** with   **B** against   **C** about   **D** over

6   **A** judging   **B** according   **C** concerning   **D** following

7   **A** result   **B** reason   **C** purpose   **D** product

8   **A** supply   **B** suggest   **C** offer   **D** propose

9   **A** possible   **B** likely   **C** hopeful   **D** welcome

10   **A** opinion   **B** attitude   **C** view   **D** position

11   **A** trust   **B** believe   **C** depend   **D** hope

12   **A** goes   **B** falls   **C** comes   **D** turns

13   **A** opposite   **B** next   **C** other   **D** far

14   **A** regard   **B** respect   **C** suppose   **D** think

15   **A** get up   **B** get on   **C** get out   **D** get over

PART 2

*For questions **16–30**, read the text below and think of the word which best fits each space. Use only **one** word in each space. There is an example at the beginning (**0**).*

*Write your word **on the separate answer sheet**.*

Example:

0	*their*	0

A BUSY FAMILY

In the front room of **(0)** …. home, the Henry family gathered around their TV set **(16)** …. a popular soap opera began. 'Look, there's Mum!' shouted 11-year-old Kathy, pointing **(17)** …. the screen. 'She's sitting at that table **(18)** …. the corner.' Sure enough, there was Julia Henry, enjoying a relaxed drink in **(19)** …. of the country's most famous TV programmes.

Julia's family see **(20)** …. unusual in her job **(21)** …. a 'bit-part' actor, or 'extra', because they are all doing it. Her husband, Tony, **(22)** …. been in several drama series as **(23)** …. as numerous adverts, while Kathy and her 13-year-old brother, Robin, have also appeared **(24)** …. TV countless times.

It all started four years **(25)** …. when Tony, an amateur actor from Lancashire, decided to leave his job and take **(26)** …. acting professionally. At the age of 41, it was a big step to take, but he has **(27)** …. regrets about it at all. Soon the whole family were being offered chances to play small parts just like him, though Tony admits there are times when he wishes he **(28)** …. a star. 'We really enjoy our lives,' says Tony, 'although it is difficult to **(29)** …. plans. A couple of phone calls can turn our week upside down, but we love **(30)** …. minute of it!'

PART 3

For questions **31–40**, *complete the second sentence so that it has a similar meaning to the first sentence, using the word given.* **Do not change the word given**. *You must use between two and five words, including the word given. There is an example at the beginning* (**0**).

Write **only** *the missing words* **on the separate answer sheet.**

Example:

0   The tennis star ignored her coach's advice.
   attention

   The tennis star didn't .... her coach's advice.

The gap can be filled by the words 'pay any attention to' so you write:

0	*pay any attention to*	0	0 1 2

---

31   I'd rather not spend another day at the beach.
   feel

   I .... another day at the beach.

32   I've never seen a match as good as this before.
   match

   This is the .... seen.

33   The staff in that office all have great respect for their boss.
   look

   The staff in that office all .... their boss.

34   'Is there anything you want from the shops?' Alison asked her mother.
   there

   Alison asked her mother if .... from the shops.

35   Sally might not bring her camera to the party, so I'll take mine.
   in

   I'll take my camera to the party .... bring hers.

36 We missed the turning because we forgot to take a map with us.
remembered

If .... a map with us, we wouldn't have missed the turning.

37 June was sure there were no mistakes in her homework.
nothing

June was sure .... with her homework.

38 Although the weather changed, the picnic went ahead as planned.
spite

The picnic went ahead as planned .... in the weather.

39 I advise you to think carefully before accepting William's offer.
better

You .... carefully before accepting William's offer.

40 Jackie hasn't been swimming for five years.
swimming

The last .... was five years ago.

PART 4

*For questions **41–55**, read the text below and look carefully at each line. Some of the lines are correct, and some have a word which should not be there. If a line is correct, put a tick (✓) by the number **on the separate answer sheet**. If a line has a word which should **not** be there, write the word **on the separate answer sheet**. There are two examples at the beginning (**0** and **00**).*

Examples:

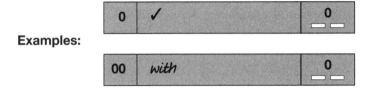

A DIFFERENCE OF OPINION

0	A musician friend of mine once went on an English course during his
00	summer holidays. What he really wanted to do was to improve with his
41	ability to think and react quickly and correctly in the spoken English.
42	He said speaking in a foreign language always made him nervous, even if
43	after three years of study. It turned out so that one of the teachers on the
44	course had very strong views on music, and was not afraid to express
45	them in the lessons. He claimed that music it was a drug, just like alcohol
46	or cigarettes, and people who could not live through their lives without it
47	were to be pitied. Whatever was the subject of the lesson, the teacher
48	always managed to include in some reference to this idea. You can
49	imagine that my friend was not very impressed. In the end, he lost his
50	temper, and spent most of the remaining lessons for arguing about music
51	and its role in people's lives. When his course had finished, he came
52	home still being angry about the experience. However, whether he
53	has enjoyed the course or not, my friend had to admit that the teacher's
54	technique had worked ever since his nervousness in English had completely
55	disappeared and he was speaking far more fluently than before.

PART 5

*For questions **56–65**, read the text below. Use the word given in capitals at the end of each line to form a word that fits in the space in the same line. There is an example at the beginning (**0**). Write your word **on the separate answer sheet**.*

Example: | 0 | *existence* | 0 |

THE HISTORY OF TOYS

When did the first toys come into **(0)** …. and what led to their **(56)** …. ? Did they represent an attempt by adults to make children happy, or did they arise from the various playful **(57)** …. of children themselves? As everyone knows, the young **(58)** …. copy the **(59)** …. of their elders, and, in their play, they often adopt objects used by adults for entirely different purposes. These objects **(60)** …. the child's **(61)** …. and lead to games in which everyday articles often play unusual and **(62)** …. roles.

EXIST
DEVELOP
ACTIVE
FREQUENT
BEHAVE
COURAGE
IMAGINE
EXPECT

It is rather surprising that for an **(63)** …. of the origin of toys, we cannot turn to folk stories. However, no traditional tale **(64)** …. to the origin of toys exists, and so our **(65)** …. is restricted to archaeological study and limited evidence from documents.

EXPLAIN
RELATE
KNOW

PAPER 4   LISTENING (approximately 40 minutes)

PART 1

You'll hear people talking in eight different situations.
*For questions **1–8**, choose the best answer **A**, **B** or **C**.*

1   Listen to these colleagues talking.
    Why is the man going to Amsterdam?

    A   on a business trip

    B   for a short holiday

    C   to study art

2   You're in a shop when you hear one of the assistants talking.
    What is he trying to do?

    A   persuade someone

    B   explain something

    C   correct a wrong idea

3   You hear this reporter on the radio.
    Who is she going to meet?

    A   a fisherman

    B   a scientist

    C   a farmer

4   Listen to this teacher talking to a student.
    What is he giving?

    A   some advice

    B   an opinion

    C   some information

5 You hear this critic talking about an exhibition.
What is its subject?

   A life in a city

   B the work of an architect

   C rich and poor countries

	5

6 You are listening to the news on the radio.
Why was Brian Bolter on trial?

   A for illegal gambling

   B for accepting bribes

   C for bribing players

	6

7 You are on a bus when you hear this passenger get on.
What does the driver offer to do?

   A tell her when the bus reaches her stop

   B point out the library

   C stop outside the library

	7

8 Listen to this boy talking about the town he lives in.
What does he feel about it?

   A He likes it.

   B It's boring.

   C It's old-fashioned.

	8

PART 2

You will hear a radio journalist interviewing Frank Irvine, a successful potter.
For questions **9–18**, complete the notes. You will need to write a word or a short phrase.

Frank Irvine

Exhibition now at [9 _____] *in North London*

Early life

Born 1948

Taken to Scotland because [10 _____] *was there*

As young child mainly interested in [11 _____]

Planned a career designing [12 _____]

Went to Edinburgh to study [13 _____]

Met wife Carole in a [14 _____] *in India*

His work

At first tried varying the type of [15 _____] *which he used*

Experimented with high [16 _____] *to get unusual effects*

In order to produce big images made [17 _____]

Later on made bigger ones for use [18 _____]

PART 3

You will hear five people being interviewed about how they spend their free time. For questions **19–23**, *choose from the list of activities* **A–F**. *Use the letters only once. There is one extra letter which you do not need to use.*

A singing

B walking

C acting

D swimming

E drawing

F cooking

Speaker 1		19
Speaker 2		20
Speaker 3		21
Speaker 4		22
Speaker 5		23

PART 4

You will hear part of a radio documentary about running a small business.
For questions **24–30**, *decide whether the idea was stated or not and mark* **Y** *for Yes, or* **N** *for No.*

24   John believes that some people are incapable of managing a business.

	24

25   Sally got advice from her father.

	25

26   Megan's business nearly failed.

	26

27   John admits that banks may cause problems for small businesses.

	27

28   Colin admits that he failed to keep his bank fully informed.

	28

29   A chance meeting helped Colin's business.

	29

30   John believes that a small business needs a computer to be efficient.

	30

PAPER 5   SPEAKING (14 minutes)

Part 1

You tell the examiner about yourself. The examiner may ask you questions such as: Where are you from? How do you usually spend your free time? What are your plans for the future? Your partner does the same.

Part 2

The examiner gives you two pictures to look at and asks you to talk about them for about a minute. Your partner does the same with two different pictures.

Part 3

The examiner gives you a photograph or drawing to look at with your partner. You are asked to solve a problem or come to a decision about something in the picture. For example, you might be asked to decide which of two rooms should be used as a study area and which as a leisure area. You discuss the problem together.

Part 4

You are asked more questions connected with your discussion in Part 3. For example, you may be asked to talk about the best ways of studying.

Practice Test 4

PAPER 1 READING (1 hour 15 minutes)

PART 1

You are going to read a newspaper article about computers. Choose from the list (A–I) the sentence which best summarises each part (1–7) of the article. There is one extra sentence which you do not need to use. There is an example at the beginning (0).
Mark your answers **on the separate answer sheet.**

A	It is uncertain whether computers should take the credit for what they can do.
B	The next computers may operate in a similar way to the human brain.
C	Human beings are no longer necessary in some situations.
D	It is unlikely that computers will ever completely replace human beings.
E	Computers can perform better than a human brain.
F	Computers have more accurate memories than human beings.
G	Human beings and computers use different methods to decide what they should do.
H	There are certain things a computer must be able to do before it can be called 'intelligent'.
I	The expectations of what computers can do have changed over the years.

Unable to think about it

0	*I*

MACHINES which seem to think have become a regular feature of our lives. Tasks that 20 years ago would have been unthinkable are now simple for quite basic computers.

1	

The most complex computers can boast remarkable achievements. Automatic pilots fly jumbo jets, and at the most sophisticated airports such as Heathrow even the largest jets can now land in zero visibility, relying entirely on computers.

2	

Chess is another field where the machine's advances go far beyond mankind's. The most advanced computers are now a match for all but the very best players and it won't be long before they will be capable of beating the champions.

3	

But is it enough for us to describe these machines as intelligent, or are their achievements in reality just a success for the scientists who have programmed them to perform a series of tasks rapidly and efficiently?

4	

Different people use the term 'artificial intelligence' to mean different things. But before it can be argued successfully that we are in the presence of an artificial intelligence, we have to prove that a machine can – as a minimum – 'learn' from the environment, independently of its programmer.

5	

One important difference between computers and the human brain is that computers rely on 'serial processing'. The fact that a computer may be able to win a complex game like chess simply reflects its ability to look at numerous possible series of moves at rapid speed and to 'learn' not to make losing moves. While this does show advanced programming, it does not show that the computer is learning independently of its programming and does not therefore show that it is intelligent. Quite apart from its ability to be influenced by the environment, the human brain differs from even the most advanced computer in that it operates with so-called 'parallel processing', doing several things at once.

6	

Sir Clive Sinclair, one of the original computer experts, is convinced that parallel processing programs for computers will be with us soon, and that these will totally change society. With parallel processing, computers would be expected to 'learn' better from their experiences and perhaps, be able to pass on the fruits of such learning to other computers, each in turn becoming more advanced. Thus could be born a generation of computers able to offer at least a more realistic attempt at intelligence.

7	

Robots are already able to do all sorts of repetitive tasks currently performed by human beings. But the effective control remains with the human brain. No computer has yet been invented which can cope with the details of human language. And the idea of an artificial intelligence with a sense of humour and a conscience still seems a faraway dream. If, however, one was to believe in the faith of scientists working in the field of artificial intelligence, one would have to suspect that dreams just could become reality.

PART 2

*You are going to read an article about a famous cook called Delia Smith. For questions **8–14**, choose the answer (**A, B, C** or **D**) which you think fits best according to the text.*
*Mark your answers **on the separate answer sheet**.*

TAKE ONE COOK ...

WATCHING HER fingers as they arrange some greenery on a plateful of pasta in a London photographic studio, it is difficult to imagine that there was ever a different Delia
5 *Smith to the confident, no-nonsense broadcaster who taught Britain how to feel good in the kitchen.*

Behind the brown-framed glasses, eyes twinkle with amusement. 'In the early
10 days I wrote the script and learnt it parrot-fashion – when filming started, my hands were shaking so much that close-ups were out of the question.' 'Those early days' were the first ten-minute afternoon programmes
15 with which the young author of a daily food column in the *London Evening Standard* made her first TV appearance exactly 21 years ago this Monday.

Judged not by her personality or
20 entertainment value, but by the test of the millions of amateurs who copy everything she does and take in every word, she was to become queen of TV cooks. An overstatement? Who else could cause an
25 invasion of the country's chemists, leaving their shelves empty of liquid glucose, simply by suggesting it as the secret ingredient of the perfect chocolate cake? Or single-handedly create a national shortage of
30 cherry brandy by pouring a drop or two into a Creole pudding? We've followed her tastes

slavishly, from her preference for freshly-milled black pepper in 1973 to her love for limes in her last book, and Britain's super-markets have responded magnificently.

Such power is impressive. It all began, in the finest traditions of stars-in-the-making, with an eleventh-hour change of mind. Looking for a new cookery presenter back in 1973, the BBC chose an American, Julia Child, but decided she was a touch too transatlantic. Would Delia Smith be interested in taking her place? She popped in, did a ten-minute test programme and waited for the result. Opinions varied, but BBC1 controller Paul Fox liked it and signed her up for the programme *Family Fare*. The budget was so low there was no allowance for film editing. If anything went wrong, the whole dish had to be started again from the beginning.

The TV success continued with a three-part cookery course, *One is Fun!*, then a Christmas series and a series called *Summer Collection*. And as Delia Smith's public acceptance has grown into something not far short of worship, so the suspicions of fellow professionals are less disguised. Who is this popular cook with the boldness to make cooking look easy?

At 54 and with nine television series and an astonishing eight million book sales behind her, she makes no excuses. Cooking, she insists, is meant to be easy. Whenever friends have expressed nervousness about inviting her and her journalist husband to dinner, she always says: 'If I can do it, then you certainly can!'

She has come a long way from the difficulties of her first TV show. She no longer learns the script by heart and now films in a specially-built conservatory in her Suffolk home. So has it all become really easy? 'The light outside keeps changing, planes fly overhead at all the wrong moments and the making of each programme is still very complicated,' she says. 'But I know one thing. I'd far rather cook for television than give a live demonstration. Having a couple of hundred eyes looking at you would be my idea of absolute hell. Whereas doing it for one bored and sympathetic cameraman with his nose in a magazine …'

8 Delia Smith has become so successful because
   A her programmes are entertaining.
   B people can actually use her recipes.
   C she has an attractive personality.
   D she uses unusual ingredients.

9 What does 'It' refer to in line 36?
   A her interest in international cookery
   B her gift for communication
   C the change of mind
   D her TV career

10 How did her broadcasting career begin?
   A She appeared on TV in America.
   B A TV programme employed her as a late choice.
   C She helped a famous presenter on TV.
   D Her test programme was liked by everyone.

11 What do her fellow professionals think of her?
  A They are ashamed of her.
  B They think her recipes are too simple.
  C They think she isn't a very professional cook.
  D They don't trust her approach.

12 What is her attitude towards cooking?
  A Results depend on the cook's experience.
  B Other people's cooking is more enjoyable than your own.
  C Anyone can cook with the right recipe.
  D You should keep trying if you fail.

13 What does she say about recording programmes today?
  A She prefers recording a programme to cooking in front of an audience.
  B She would prefer to find a television crew who were interested.
  C She misses the facilities which she used at the BBC.
  D She is not as interested in TV presentations as she was.

14 How has Delia Smith changed?
  A She is more relaxed.
  B She is more amusing.
  C She no longer uses a script.
  D She is a better cook.

PART 3

*You are going to read the introduction to a guidebook about the Yosemite National Park in the USA. Eight sentences have been removed from the article. Choose from the sentences (**A–I**) the one which fits each gap (**15–21**). There is one extra sentence which you do not need to use. There is an example at the beginning (**0**).*

*Mark your answers **on the separate answer sheet**.*

YOSEMITE NATIONAL PARK

WHAT exactly is Yosemite? Is it Bridalveil Fall thundering and pouring in early June? Is it a long summer's day at Tuolumne Meadows? Is it the ice-carved, rocky world of the high Sierra seen from Glacier Point?

| 0 | *I* | It is an energetic walk over the Four Mile Trail. It is the smell of pine trees at Hogdon Meadow campground. It might also be a walk among some of the largest trees in the world. Our list could go on and on.

| 15 | | Roaring waterfalls, falling hundreds of feet, fascinate even the most bored traveler. Shining walls of towering rockface challenge the skills of hundreds of mountain climbers and capture the eyes and minds of thousands of visitors. Yosemite's rushing mountain streams, alpine landscape, forests and all the rest of its natural features combine to make this national park unique in the opinion of nearly every observer.

| 16 | | These earlier

inhabitants of the region left traces of a lifestyle which depended upon the use of local plants and animals. Remains of that culture, on display in museums and books, sometimes seen in the surfaces of rock, recalled mainly in names upon the land, show us people's lives which were directly connected to this region.

17 [blank] From the earliest Spanish explorers who gave names to the general region, to the fur trappers, miners and others who came seeking paths through the Sierra Nevada or hoping for personal gain, Yosemite displays an exciting past which helps us understand the present. It is a story filled with characters who were impressed enough to stay, advertise, exploit and preserve.

18 [blank] Its geologic features are the product of time's hidden forces, carved out by glaciers and streams. Its birds and bears delight suburban America. Its buzzing mosquitoes remind us that we are not in a shopping mall. Its flower-filled meadows and tall forests remind us of the sheep and loggers who once looked out upon this scene.

19 [blank] While preserved for all to enjoy, perhaps not everyone can enjoy it at once. Occasionally crowded conditions disturb many first-time visitors. Yosemite Valley does not seem like the quiet place generally shown in photographs. An ever-increasing, demanding public raises the question – can any national park be all things to all people?

20 [blank] Bicycling in Yosemite alley, walking the John Muir Trail, skiing at Badger Pass or sitting quietly beside the Merced River are all possibilities. One can walk with freedom in the park, allowing closer examination of the natural surroundings. Alternatively, visitors to Yosemite can take shuttle buses and disembark for short adventures beyond the roadway or can go into informational museums.

Yosemite is a spectacular Sierra Nevada park. Yosemite is history, geology, Indians, scenery beyond compare, and conservation. Yosemite is part of America that we always want to experience and never want to lose. It has become a part of our imagination. We search in Yosemite for what we have not been able to find elsewhere.

21 [blank] And that may explain why Yosemite is so popular.

A Yosemite recalls a history, rich with colorful personalities and filled with dramatic events.

B Because of that, Yosemite is more than a park, it is an ideal.

C Yosemite contains natural features which cannot fail to attract human attention.

D Yosemite is also an example of wild America, in contrast to the America outside its boundaries.

E For today's visitors, Yosemite offers a source of pleasure and a choice of activity.

F Yosemite is well-known not just to Americans, but to people all over the world.

G Yosemite might also be an example of a national park that is too successful, that has become too popular.

H Yosemite also shows us how the original native American people lived.

I Obviously, Yosemite is all of these things and much, much more.

PART 4

*You are going to read a magazine article about beauty. For questions **22–34**, choose from the people in the box (**A–G**). There is an example at the beginning (**0**). For question **35**, choose the answer (**A, B, C** or **D**) which you think fits best according to the text.*
*Mark your answers **on the separate answer sheet**.*

A	Alfred Linney
B	Mark Lowey
C	Sir Francis Galton
D	David Perrett
E	Francis Bacon
F	Judith Langlois
G	Michael Cunningham

Which person states or stated the following opinion?

A happy expression can be of particular importance.	**0**	*G*
Some beautiful faces have features which are unacceptable in an ordinary face.	**22**	
A judgement of whether a female face is attractive or not will vary according to women's position in that society.	**23**	
Ideas of beauty are not limited by nationality.	**24**	
When choosing someone for a job, an employer may focus on particular features in a face.	**25**	
We can recognise a beautiful face when we are very young.	**26**	
A definition of a beautiful face does not exist.	**27**	
Making individual characteristics stronger can make a face more attractive.	**28**	

Features combined from several people are an improvement on individual faces.

29	

The most beautiful women do not look similar to each other.

30	

Women who look older are treated with more consideration.

31	

A face which has completely regular features can never be really beautiful.

32	

Some features are thought suitable in one situation but not in another.

33	

Beautiful faces share some of the same types of features.

34	

35   What is the writer trying to do?
   A   explain the different reactions to beautiful faces
   B   set out some of the different theories about beauty
   C   come to a conclusion about what is a beautiful face
   D   explain why people are interested in beauty

Perfect beauty

It's not all a matter of taste – and that's official. But we may be no nearer to learning just what beauty really is.

WE ALL recognise beauty when we see it, but what makes a beautiful face is something that few can agree on. The most controversial finding in some research carried out by **Dr Alfred Linney** of University College Hospital is that there is no such thing as *the* beautiful face. Instead, Linney has found that the features of most top fashion models are just as varied as those of everyone else. 'Some have teeth that stick out, some have a long face, and others a jutting chin. There is no one ideal of beauty that they are all a bit closer to,' he says.

One of Linney's co-workers, orthodontist **Mark Lowey**, even considered that some of the models' features might have required surgery if found on a 'normal' face. 'One type of problem people often seek help for is teeth that stick out,' he says. 'One of the models has teeth that stick out eight millimetres and she still looks lovely.'

Recent findings from UCH go against one of the most influential scientific ideas of beauty – that the combination of the features of several ordinary faces can result in one beautiful face. The theory dates back to the last century and is the work of **Sir Francis Galton**, who made his name both as a psychologist and geneticist. In 1878 he discovered that if photographs of a number of faces were put on top of each other, most people considered the resulting face to be more beautiful than the faces which made them.

But this theory has taken a knock in a recent report from the science magazine *Nature*. **Dr David Perrett**, of the University of St Andrews, combined some photographs of both European and Japanese faces and asked people to judge them. 'We found that not only were individual attractive faces preferred to the combined ones, but that when we used the computer to emphasise the combined features away from the average, that too was preferred,' he said. This would account for the popularity of actresses such as Brigitte Nielsen and Daryl Hannah, who have features that are far from average.

The research also gives scientific respectability to another old idea. As the philosopher **Francis Bacon** put it more than three centuries ago: 'There is no excellent beauty which does not have some strangeness in the proportion.'

Dr David Perrett claims, however, that his beautiful faces had something in common. 'The more attractive ones had higher cheek bones, a thinner jaw, and larger eyes relative to the size of the face than the average ones did,' he says. He also found that beauty can go across cultures: the Japanese found the same European faces beautiful as the Europeans did, and vice versa. According to **Dr Judith Langlois** of the University of Texas, even three-month-old babies prefer beautiful faces to plainer ones.

Another beauty researcher, **Dr Michael Cunningham** of Elmhurst College, Illinois, has been looking at the effect of individual features in a beautiful face and has discovered that some features may or may not be desirable, depending on what the judge is looking for. When male interviewers are selecting a woman for a job, for instance, arched expressive eyebrows and dilated pupils are seen as desirable. On the other hand, men looking for a partner with a view to settling down and starting a family, found a wide smile more important than aggressive eyes and eyebrows. Cunningham also found that attractive women with mature features, such as small eyes and a large nose, received more respect. 'It could be that societies where women have more power and independence idealise women with more mature features,' he says, 'while those which value dependent, weak females may prefer baby faces.'

But the search for a better definition of beauty will continue, driven by the billion-pound beauty industry's desire to find new ways of closing the gap between the actual and the ideal.

PAPER 2   WRITING (1 hour 30 minutes)

PART 1

You **must** *answer this question.*

1   You are in England helping to organise a course for foreign students which begins next week. This morning you received a message from Katarina Tabacek, one of the students who has reserved a place on the course. She wants to bring a friend with her on the course. Look at the description of the course below and the notes you have made and write to Katarina explaining why her friend cannot come on the course.

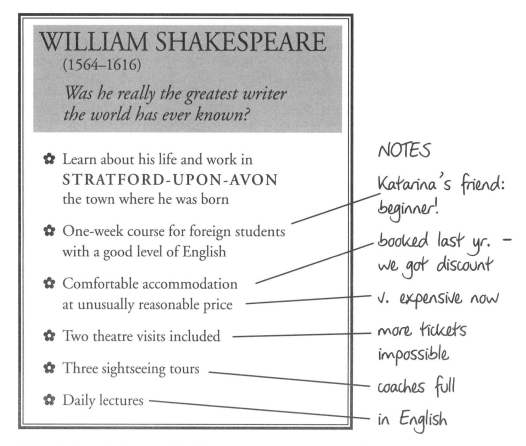

Write a **letter** of between **120–180** words in an appropriate style on the next page. Do not write any addresses.

PART 1

....
....
....
....
....
....
....
....
....
....
....
....
....
....
....
....
....
....
....
....
....
....
....
....
....
....
....
....

PART 2

Write an answer to **one** *of the questions* **2–5** *in this part. Write your answer in* **120–180** *words in an appropriate style on the next page, putting the question number in the box.*

2   You have decided to write a letter to a friend or relative while on holiday in a place you have not visited before.

Write your **letter**, describing your first impressions of the place and people. Do not write any addresses.

3   Your teacher has asked you to write a short story which finishes with the sentence: **I promised myself there and then that I would never set foot in that place again**.

Write your **story**.

4

> ## *Television Weekly* wants to hear from you!
>
> If the quality of modern television annoys you, here's your chance to let us know why. We'll publish the best articles from readers on the subject:
> **The problem with today's TV programmes**.

Write your **article** for the magazine.

5   **Background reading texts**

Answer **one** of the following two questions based on your reading of **one** of the set books (see p. v). Write the title of the book next to the question number box.

Either   **(a)**   Describe any moments in the book which you find especially interesting and say why.

or   **(b)**   If you could choose to be one of the characters in the book, who would you choose and why?

PART 2

Question	

....
....
....
....
....
....
....
....
....
....
....
....
....
....
....
....
....
....
....
....
....
....
....
....
....
....
....
....
....
....
....
....

PAPER 3 USE OF ENGLISH (1 hour 15 minutes)

PART 1

For questions **1–15***, read the text below and decide which answer* **A**, **B**, **C** *or* **D** *best fits each space. There is an example at the beginning* (**0**).
Mark your answers **on the separate answer sheet**.

Example:

0   **A** does   **B** do   **C** have   **D** had

```
 0 |   A     B     C     D
   |   ▬     ▭     ▭     ▭
```

DREAMS

Everyone can dream. Indeed, everyone **(0)** …. dream. Those who **(1)** …. that they never dream at all actually dream **(2)** …. as frequently as the rest of us, **(3)** …. they may not remember anything about it. Even those of us who are perfectly **(4)** …. of dreaming night **(5)** …. night very seldom remember those dreams in **(6)** …. detail but merely retain an untidy mixture of seemingly unrelated impressions. Dreams are not simply visual – we dream with all our **(7)** …. , so that we appear to experience sound, touch, smell, and taste.

One of the world's oldest **(8)** …. written documents is the Egyptian *Book of Dreams*. This volume is about five thousand years old, so you can **(9)** …. that dreams were believed to have a special significance even then. Many ancient civilisations believed that you **(10)** …. never wake a sleeping person as, during sleep, the soul had left the body and might not be able to return **(11)** …. time if the sleeper were suddenly **(12)** …. .

From ancient times to the present **(13)** …. , people have been **(14)** …. attempts to interpret dreams and to explain their significance. There are many books available on the subject of dream interpretation, although unfortunately there are almost as many meanings for a particular dream **(15)** …. there are books.

1 **A** demand   **B** promise   **C** agree   **D** claim

2 **A** also   **B** just   **C** only   **D** quite

3 **A** though   **B** besides   **C** however   **D** despite

4 **A** familiar   **B** accustomed   **C** aware   **D** used

5 **A** after   **B** on   **C** through   **D** over

6 **A** great   **B** high   **C** strong   **D** deep

7 **A** feelings   **B** emotions   **C** impressions **D** senses

8 **A** considered   **B** known   **C** regarded   **D** estimated

9 **A** see   **B** feel   **C** ensure   **D** think

10 **A** would   **B** ought   **C** should   **D** need

11 **A** by   **B** in   **C** with   **D** for

12 **A** awoke   **B** awoken   **C** awake   **D** awaken

13 **A** minute   **B** hour   **C** moment   **D** day

14 **A** doing   **B** putting   **C** making   **D** taking

15 **A** as   **B** like   **C** so   **D** such

PART 2

For questions **16–30**, *read the text below and think of the word which best fits each space. Use only* **one** *word in each space. There is an example at the beginning* (**0**).

Write your word **on the separate answer sheet**.

Example: | **0** | *is* | | **0** | ▭ ▭ |

THE EXPORT OF ICE

Ice from the Rocky Mountains in the United States **(0)** …. being exported to countries on the other **(16)** …. of the world. From Seattle to Tokyo **(17)** …. seem a long way to send ice, but the idea is certainly not new. **(18)** …. early as 1833, Frederick Tudor, **(19)** …. as the 'Ice King', sent a shipload of ice from America to India. About half **(20)** …. ice melted during the long journey, but Tudor would have **(21)** …. a profit even **(22)** …. he had lost three quarters of his cargo.

Most people think **(23)** …. ice as rather short-lived but, when it was cut from frozen lakes in huge blocks and stored in the depths of a sailing ship, **(24)** …. life was considerably extended. In Britain in the 1840s, **(25)** …. was already a local commercial ice trade, but the import of ice, first from America and then from Norway, **(26)** …. about a revolution in the food business. The main port of entry for Norwegian ice was London, from **(27)** …. the firm of Carlo Gatti, the largest dealers, distributed ice around the country. It was Gatti **(28)** …. introduced the penny ice-cream in the 1850s. **(29)** …. then, ice-cream had been a luxury, but the penny ice, served in Gatti's cafés, became a Victorian fashion and brought hundreds of Italian ice-cream sellers **(30)** …. the streets of the capital.

PART 3

*For questions **31–40**, complete the second sentence so that it has a similar meaning to the first sentence, using the word given. **Do not change the word given**. You must use between two and five words, including the word given. There is an example at the beginning (**0**).*
*Write **only** the missing words **on the separate answer sheet**.*

Example:

0   The tennis star ignored her coach's advice.
    attention

    The tennis star didn't .... her coach's advice.

The gap can be filled by the words 'pay any attention to' so you write:

0	*pay any attention to*	0	0 1 2

---

31   Martin hasn't mentioned the party to me at all.
    word

    Martin hasn't .... about the party.

32   Apparently, Sheila wasn't listening to me.
    appear

    Sheila .... listening to me.

33   Margaret was offered a place on the course but couldn't accept because she was ill.
    turn

    Margaret was offered a place on the course but ....
    because she was ill.

34   'I wouldn't trust Frank with your money if I were you, Carl,' I said.
    advised

    I .... Frank with his money.

35   I don't know Lesley's reasons for resigning.
    idea

    I .... Lesley resigned.

36 Have you any desks in stock which are cheaper than this?
   desk

   Is this .... in stock?

37 Teams of experts were examining the damage to the building.
   examined

   The damage to the building .... teams of experts.

38 Joe's father used to insist that he washed the car at the weekend.
   make

   Joe's father used to .... the car at the weekend.

39 I wish John still wrote to me.
   miss

   I .... from John.

40 Everyone thinks Alan will accept the job within the next few days.
   expected

   Alan .... the job within the next few days.

PART 4

*For questions **41–55**, read the text below and look carefully at each line. Some of the lines are correct, and some have a word which should not be there. If a line is correct, put a tick (✓) by the number **on the separate answer sheet**. If a line has a word which should not be there, write the word **on the separate answer sheet**. There are two examples at the beginning (**0** and **00**).*

Examples:

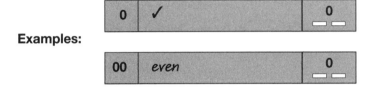

0	✓	0

00	*even*	0

IS LETTER-WRITING A LOST ART?

0	Do you write letters any more? In this age of advanced telephone
00	networks and electronic mail, it seems that fewer and even fewer people are
41	taking the time to sit down and write letters to friends and relatives. For
42	hundreds of past years, letters were the only way to keep in touch with
43	people who were at any distance away, and letter-writing was seen as an
44	important skill for all those educated people to master. Gradually, however,
45	the importance of letter-writing has decreased up to a point where the majority
46	of us must have to make a special effort to turn out something worthwhile when
47	we apply for a job or make a complaint. Personal letters, just when we
48	bother to write them at all, are often not much more than a stream of
49	unconnected thoughts. In business circles, the same tendency is for routine
50	communications to become shorter and, although clients they may
51	appreciate a detailed letter, an employee who sends out long letters is often
52	regarded as an inefficient. Many people prefer the telephone in all
53	circumstances and, naturally, its own speed is vital in many situations but
54	how very often have you put the phone down, dissatisfied with what you
55	have managed to say? I don't think I'll throw my pen away from yet.

For questions **56–65**, *read the text below. Use the word given in capitals at the end of each line to form a word that fits in the space in the same line. There is an example at the beginning (**0**). Write your word* **on the separate answer sheet**.

Example:

0	*painting*	0 __ __

A CHANGE OF CAREER

Wildlife **(0)** …. had always been a hobby for Mark Chester, but   **PAINT**
when he lost his job, he took the **(56)** …. to turn it into a full-time   **DECIDE**
career. Mark had obtained his **(57)** …. qualifications in the fields of   **PROFESSION**
(58) …. and advertising and felt that these skills would be useful in his   **PHOTOGRAPH**
new life. He had sold his work before, and was **(59)** …. confident that   **REASON**
he could earn enough to live on.

Mark discovered that he would be able to receive an **(60)** …. from a   **ALLOW**
government **(61)** …. to help him set up his business. They also   **AGENT**
provided him with **(62)** …. information on how to run his affairs.   **USE**
As **(63)** …. of his work increased, Mark realised that he could not   **SELL**
paint enough **(64)** …. pictures to keep up with demand, so he is now   **ORIGIN**
trying to interest a **(65)** …. in producing prints of his work. Meanwhile,   **PUBLISH**
Mark has started making prints of his own.

PAPER 4   LISTENING (approximately 40 minutes)

PART 1

You will hear people talking in eight different situations.
*For questions **1–8**, choose the best answer **A**, **B** or **C**.*

1   You hear this man talking on the radio about a politician.
   When did he get to know her?

   A   at school

   B   at university

   C   in his first job

	1

2   You're in a restaurant when you overhear this conversation.
   What is wrong with the food?

   A   It's stale.

   B   It's overcooked.

   C   It's the wrong order.

	2

3   You hear the weather forecast on the radio.
   How long will the bad weather last?

   A   until midday tomorrow

   B   until tomorrow evening

   C   until the day after tomorrow

	3

4   You are in a bank when you hear this conversation.
   What does the woman want to do?

   A   borrow some money

   B   take out some of her money

   C   transfer her money to a new account

	4

5 Listen to this man describing a concert.
   What did he like about it?

   A   the first part

   B   the songs

   C   the instrumental section

6 Listen to these language teachers.
   What may cause a problem for students, according to the woman?

   A   violence

   B   prejudice

   C   loneliness

7 Some friends are talking about a film.
   What does the boy emphasise about the director?

   A   She's Indian.

   B   She's a woman.

   C   She's young.

8 You hear this woman talking about a colleague on the phone.
   What has he done?

   A   passed his driving test

   B   bought a car

   C   started driving lessons

PART 2

You will hear a radio feature about the city of Bristol.
*For questions **9–18**, complete the notes. You will need to write a word or a short phrase.*

Bristol

Ashton Court

[9] miles from centre

Visitor Centre has display about 100 years

of [10]

Museums

In [11] area

Industrial Museum

Many examples of things to do with [12]

S.S. Great Britain

An early ship made of [13]

Bristol Zoo

Special events include displays, treasure hunts, and an

exhibition of [14] of wildlife

For little children, there's the [15]

For bigger children, there's the [16]

The Exploratory

Opportunity to learn about many aspects

of [17]

Variety of shows, including 'Bubble Magic'

and [18]

PART 3

You will hear five people talking about feelings they have experienced.
For questions 19–23, choose from the list of feelings A–F. Use the letters only
once. There is one extra letter which you do not need to use.

A guilt

B anger

C fear

D homesickness

E shyness

F embarrassment

Speaker 1		19
Speaker 2		20
Speaker 3		21
Speaker 4		22
Speaker 5		23

PART 4

You will hear part of a radio interview with Sharon Walker, a young woman who has recently changed her career.
For questions 24–30 decide whether the statements are true or false and mark **T** *for True, or* **F** *for False.*

24	Sharon gave up professional tennis three years ago.	24

25	She still enjoys playing.	25

26	When she was young, she was amused by newspaper reports about her.	26

27	She says that journalists invented stories about her love life.	27

28	She was criticised by some other players when she retired.	28

29	She has been feeling unfulfilled since she retired.	29

30	It's unimportant to her how well Maisie plays tennis.	30

PAPER 5   SPEAKING (14 minutes)

Part 1

You tell the examiner about yourself. The examiner may ask you questions such as: Where are you from? How do you usually spend your free time? What are your plans for the future? Your partner does the same.

Part 2

The examiner gives you two pictures to look at and asks you to talk about them for about a minute. Your partner does the same with two different pictures.

Part 3

The examiner gives you a photograph or drawing to look at with your partner. You are asked to solve a problem or come to a decision about something in the picture. For example, you might be asked to decide which of two rooms should be used as a study area and which as a leisure area. You discuss the problem together.

Part 4

You are asked more questions connected with your discussion in Part 3. For example, you may be asked to talk about the best ways of studying.

CAMBRIDGE
EXAMINATIONS, CERTIFICATES AND DIPLOMAS
ENGLISH AS A FOREIGN LANGUAGE

University of Cambridge
Local Examinations Syndicate
International Examinations

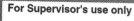

Examination Details	9999/01 99/D99
Examination Title	First Certificate in English
Centre/Candidate No.	AA999/9999
Candidate Name	A.N. EXAMPLE

• Sign here if the details above are correct

X

• Tell the Supervisor now if the details above
are not correct

Candidate Answer Sheet: FCE Paper 1 Reading

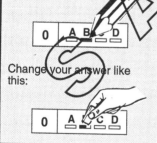

Use a pencil

Mark ONE letter for each
question.

For example, if you think **B** is
the right answer to the
question, mark your answer
sheet like this:

0	A **B** C D

Change your answer like
this:

0	A ~~B~~ C D

6	A B C D E F G H I
7	A B C D E F G H I
8	A B C D E F G H I
9	A B C D E F G H I
10	A B C D E F G H I
11	A B C D E F G H I
12	A B C D E F G H I
13	A B C D E F G H I
14	A B C D E F G H I
15	A B C D E F G H I
16	A B C D E F G H I
17	A B C D E F G H I
18	A B C D E F G H I
19	A B C D E F G H I
20	A B C D E F G H I

21	A B C D E F G H I
22	A B C D E F G H I
23	A B C D E F G H I
24	A B C D E F G H I
25	A B C D E F G H I
26	A B C D E F G H I
27	A B C D E F G H I
28	A B C D E F G H I
29	A B C D E F G H I
30	A B C D E F G H I
31	A B C D E F G H I
32	A B C D E F G H I
33	A B C D E F G H I
34	A B C D E F G H I
35	A B C D E F G H I

1	A B C D E F G H I
2	A B C D E F G H I
3	A B C D E F G H I
4	A B C D E F G H I
5	A B C D E F G H I

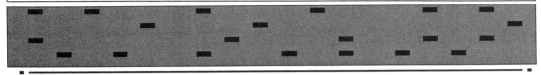

Examination Details   9999/03   99/D99

Examination Title   First Certificate in English

Centre/Candidate No.   AA999/9999

Candidate Name   A.N. EXAMPLE

• Sign here if the details above are correct

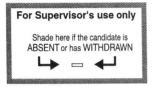

For Supervisor's use only

Shade here if the candidate is
ABSENT or has WITHDRAWN

➥ ⊟ ↵

X

• Tell the Supervisor now if the details above
  are not correct

Candidate Answer Sheet: FCE Paper 3 Use of English

Use a pencil

For **Part 1**: Mark ONE letter for each question.

For example, if you think **C** is the
right answer to the question,
mark your answer sheet like this:

For **Parts 2, 3, 4** and **5**: Write your
answers in the spaces next to the
numbers like this:

| 0 | A B C D |

| 0 | *example* |

Part 1					Part 2		Do not write here
1	A	B	C	D	16		16
2	A	B	C	D	17		17
3	A	B	C	D	18		18
4	A	B	C	D	19		19
5	A	B	C	D	20		20
6	A	B	C	D	21		21
7	A	B	C	D	22		22
8	A	B	C	D	23		23
9	A	B	C	D	24		24
10	A	B	C	D	25		25
11	A	B	C	D	26		26
12	A	B	C	D	27		27
13	A	B	C	D	28		28
14	A	B	C	D	29		29
15	A	B	C	D	30		30

Turn
over
for
Parts
3 - 5
➜

114   *You may photocopy this page.* **© UCLES/K&J**

Part 3	Do not write here		
31	31 0	1	2
32	32 0	1	2
33	33 0	1	2
34	34 0	1	2
35	35 0	1	2
36	36 0	1	2
37	37 0	1	2
38	38 0	1	2
39	39 0	1	2
40	40 0	1	2

Part 4	Do not write here
41	41
42	42
43	43
44	44
45	45
46	46
47	47
48	48
49	49
50	50
51	51
52	52
53	53
54	54
55	55

Part 5	Do not write here
56	56
57	57
58	58
59	59
60	60
61	61
62	62
63	63
64	64
65	65

CAMBRIDGE
EXAMINATIONS, CERTIFICATES AND DIPLOMAS
ENGLISH AS A FOREIGN LANGUAGE

University of Cambridge
Local Examinations Syndicate
International   Examinations

For Supervisor's use only

Shade here if the candidate is
ABSENT or has WITHDRAWN

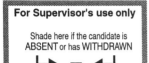

☒

Examination Details	9999/04
Examination Title	First Certificate in English
Centre/Candidate No.	AA999/9999
Candidate Name	A.N. EXAMPLE

99/D99

• Sign here if the details above are correct

• Tell the Supervisor now if the details above
  are not correct

Candidate Answer Sheet: FCE Paper 4 Listening

Mark test version below
A   B   C   D   E

Use a pencil

For **Parts 1** and **3**:
Mark ONE letter for
each question.

For example, if you
think **B** is the right
answer to the
question, mark your
answer sheet like this:

0	A B̲ C

For **Parts 2** and **4**:
Write your answers in
the spaces next to the
numbers like this:

0	*example*

Part 1

1	A	B	C
2	A	B	C
3	A	B	C
4	A	B	C
5	A	B	C
6	A	B	C
7	A	B	C
8	A	B	C

Part 2

	Do not write here
9	9
10	10
11	11
12	12
13	13
14	14
15	15
16	16
17	17
18	18

Part 3

19	A	B	C	D	E	F
20	A	B	C	D	E	F
21	A	B	C	D	E	F
22	A	B	C	D	E	F
23	A	B	C	D	E	F

Part 4

	Do not write here
24	24
25	25
26	26
27	27
28	28
29	29
30	30

You may photocopy this page.   **© UCLES/K&J**